JP

PHILIP JODIDIO

ARCHITECTURE IN JAPAN

TASCHEN

KÖLN LONDON LOS ANGELES MADRID PARIS TOKYO

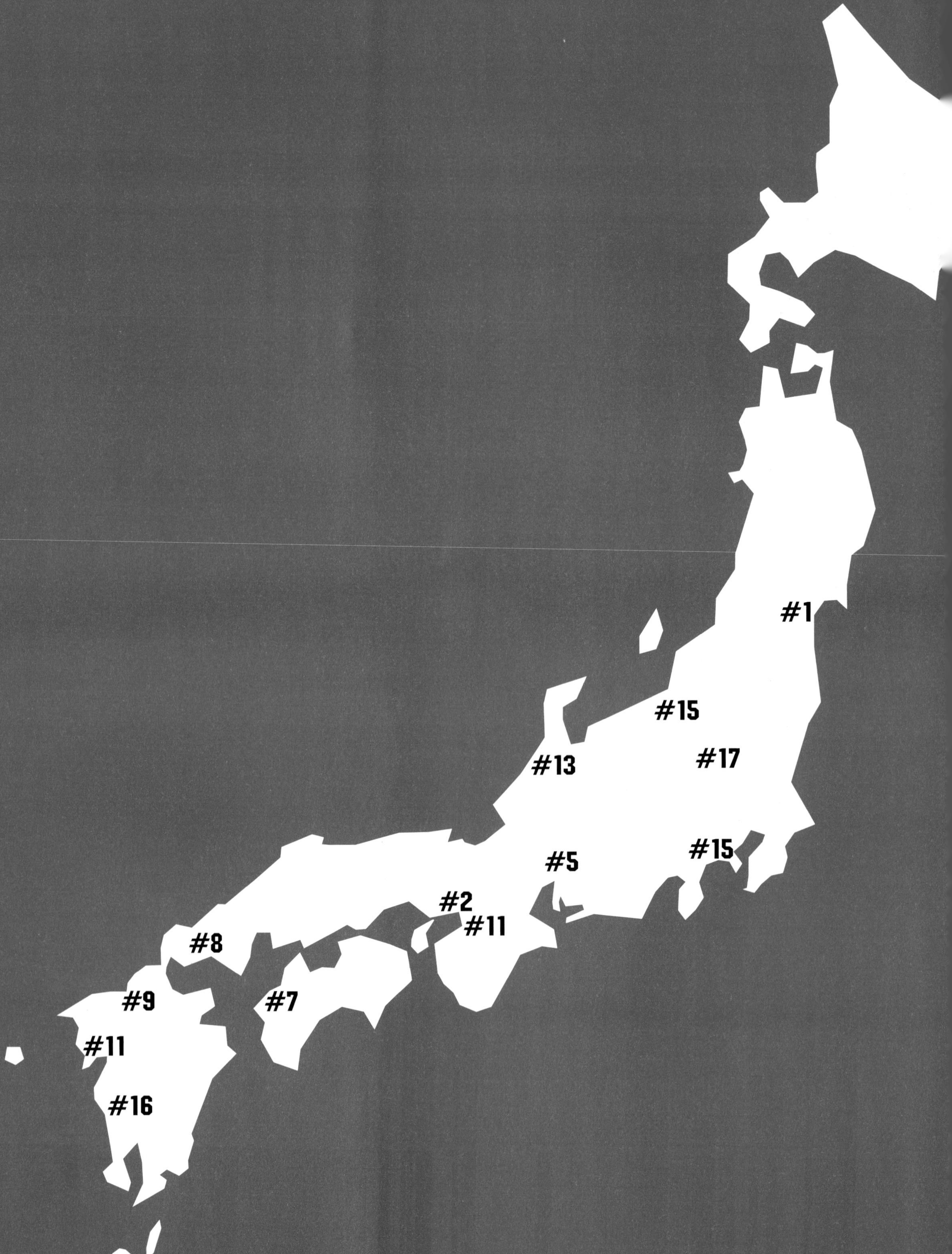
#1
#15
#17
#13
#15
#5
#2
#11
#8
#9
#7
#11
#16

TOKYO

#14

#6

#2/9/10/13

#10 #3/4/12

#4

INTRODUCTION

IN PRAISE OF AMBIGUITY

Slightly smaller than California, Japan has a much larger population, estimated at 127 417 244 in July 2005. Over the past decade, the population has increased by approximately two million people but, overall, the Japanese are aging. Certainly the largest modern city in the world, Tokyo, with only 0.6% of the total area of Japan, is home to 10% of its inhabitants, creating an extreme density of 5 655 persons per square kilometer. A large part of the eastern seaboard of the country, between Tokyo and Osaka, is almost a continuous urban area whereas, to the west, more mountainous and less densely settled areas exist. These facts, and in particular the urban density of the country, are important to understanding its architecture, particularly where residential construction is concerned. Another significant factor in Japanese architecture is the underlying sense of fragility born of catastrophes. Successive disasters, some naturales and some man-made, have shaped the contemporary face of Tokyo, for example. The first of these in the 20th-century was the Great Kanto Earthquake of 1923, measuring 7.9 on the Richter scale, which may have killed 200 000 and left 64% of the remaining population homeless. The second, even more radical in its destruction was the American firebombing of the city between March and May of 1945. More people died in these months than in the instantaneous devastation of Hiroshima. By September 1945, the population that had exceeded 6.9 million in 1942, had dropped through death and emigration to 2 777 000. Incendiary devices, dropped on a city constituted mostly of wooden structures, were particularly efficient. For this reason, it can be said that the largest city on earth has been built almost entirely since 1945. At the outset, this construction went forward with limited means. As in war-torn Europe, it was essential to build cheaply and fast. In more recent times, an implacable commercial logic, which has little to do with the canons of easthetics has been the dominant influence. In a sense, this tidal wave of bad architecture is the second man-made disaster of Tokyo's recent history. It has swept before it much of the beauty of centuries-old tradition.

The emergence of modern Japanese architecture can be viewed in terms of a progressive liberation from Western influences. When Commodore Perry viewed the city of Edo during his 1853–54 expedition, he described it as an "extensive plain with a magnificent background of mountains and wooded country." The far-reaching consequences of the Perry Expedition have often been analyzed, but it should be recalled that, as early as 1872, the Meiji government called on the British architect and planner Thomas Waters to rebuild the sector to the southeast of the Imperial Palace, destroyed in that year by fire. Along a broad avenue, Waters laid out Neoclassical buildings along what became known as the Ginza. Another Englishman, Josiah Conder (1852–1920), built numerous heavy Second Empire style masonry buildings, such as the National Museum in Ueno Park (1882), that became the symbols of the Japanese establishment until the Ministry of the Cabinet decided to call on the Germans Hermann Ende (1829–1907) and Wilhelm Böckmann (1832–1902). Their plan for a Prussian-style building for the Japanese Diet capped with a pagoda-like form met with concerted opposition, and calls for a resolution to the conflict between indigenous and Western architectural styles.[1]

"There was sixty to seventy feet of soft mud below the upper depth of eight feet of surface soil on the site. That mud seemed a merciful provision—a good cushion to relieve the terrible shocks. Why not float the building upon it? A battleship floats on salt water..."[2] This is how another foreign architect in Japan, Frank Lloyd Wright, described his plans for the Imperial Hotel in Tokyo (1916–22). Demolished in 1967, this eccentric structure famously survived the devastating earthquake of 1923, adding to Wright's reputation, not least of all in Japan.

Wright was, of course, not the only Western architect to have exerted an influence on the development of modern Japanese architecture. Le Corbusier, for example, who continues to fascinate many contemporary architects, made his presence felt through projects such as the National Museum of Western Art in Ueno Park in Tokyo (1959), and through the work of such figures as Kunio Maekawa, who worked in Le Corbusier's atelier in France from 1928 to 1930 before establishing his own office in Tokyo in 1935. Maekawa completed the 1979 addition to the National Museum of Western Art, symbolically reaffirming the importance of Le Corbusier in Japan.

On November 4, 1935, the German architect Bruno Taut (1880–1938) wrote in his journal, "I can truly claim to be the discoverer of Katsura." This affirmation, concerning the 17th-century imperial residence located near Kyoto, is of considerable importance for the evolution of contemporary Japanese architecture. Whereas the Japanese had in various ways absorbed the Western influences to which they were subjected after the Perry Expedition, they had come to reject many aspects of their own tradition. Thus the rise of fascism in Japan was accompanied by a certain rejection of Western-inspired modernity in favor of an architecture called „teikan yoshiki," or the "Imperial roof style," which featured heavy cubic structures capped by equally ungainly "Japanese" roofs. Having arrived in Japan in May 1933, Taut spent three and a half years writing about Katsura, linking its elegant simplicity to the goals of the modern movement and calling it an "eternal monument." As Arata Isozaki points out, other Western architects, such as the German Gustav Prattz, had visited Katsura even before Taut, and had integrated its lessons into "the renewal of world architecture."[3] The rediscovery of the fundamental links between the purity of Japanese tradition and modernism itself occurred only after the trauma of World War II, partially because the very idea of calling on tradition had been misappropriated by a largely discredited political ideology.

MASTERS OF THEIR ART

The postwar discovery of Japanese tradition by the Japanese themselves was aided by figures such as the architect Kenzo Tange. Born in 1913, Tange had worked in the 1930s in the office of Kunio Maekawa, but his Olympic Sports Halls for the 1964 Tokyo Olympics announced the emergence of an indigenous moder-

[1] "Order and Anarchy: Tokyo from 1868 to the Present," by William Coaldrake in "Tokyo, Form and Spirit," Walker Art Center, Harry N. Abrams, New York, 1986.

[2] Frank Lloyd Wright, "An Autobiography," Duell, Sloan and Pearce, New York, 1943.

[3] Arata Isozaki, "Katsura: A Model for Post-Modern Architecture," in "Katsura Villa – Space and Form," Iwanami Shoten Publishers, Tokyo, 1983.

nity on a par in terms of quality and inventiveness with that of the West. Author of the Hiroshima Peace Park and Museum, a moving testimony to the horrific impact of the atomic bomb, Tange, who died in 2005, remains a symbol of modern Japanese architecture though his late work, such as the Tokyo City Hall, a 243-meter-tall double tower that occupies three full blocks in the Shinju-ku area (1991), and is considered by many to be a symbol of the excesses of the bubble years.

A number of the leading figures of today's Japanese contemporary architecture scene emerged from the office of Kenzo Tange, amongst them Arata Isozaki and Yoshio Taniguchi. As it happens, both Isozaki and Taniguchi are important because they succeeded in exporting the achievements of Japan's architecture to other countries and, in particular, the United States. Isozaki has long been one of the six or seven "star" architects who straddle the globe with their projects. His Museum of Contemporary Art, Los Angeles (1981–86), was one of the first institutions to be designed by a foreign architect in the United States, and Taniguchi's more recent Museum of Modern Art reconstruction in New York shows that Japanese architects have been accepted, even within the art establishment's "inner sanctum." In the generation of Isozaki and Taniguchi, Fumihiko Maki is another figure of international importance, whose recent projects include a new tower for the United Nations in New York, or buildings for the Aga Khan in Canada. Like Taniguchi, Maki was in part educated in the United States and has a full mastery of English, which is still not the case of all of Japan's major architects. Another master born before the War is Hiroshi Hara, author of numerous very visible buildings in Japan, such as the Umeda Sky Building (Kita-ku, Osaka, 1988–93), and the massive Kyoto JR Railway Station (Sakyo-ku, Kyoto, 1990–97). Hara has also worked on numerous private houses, such as the Orimoto residence featured here, with the innovative and intelligent approach that characterizes his work.

Tadao Ando may be the best-known contemporary architect in the world, and it is indeed with Ando that Japan has reached the highest levels of international notoriety in this area. Born in Osaka in 1941, Tadao Ando was self-educated as an architect, largely through his travels in the United States, Europe and Africa (1962–69). He received the 1995 Pritzker Prize, and aside from his prodigious building in Japan, he has recently completed the Modern Art Museum of Fort Worth (1999–2002) and the Pulitzer Foundation for the Arts (St Louis, Missouri, 1997–2000). A scheme to design a museum of contemporary art in Paris for the French billionaire François Pinault was unfortunately cancelled in the spring of 2005. Ando's powerful drawings and equally strong, usually concrete buildings have been admired and imitated by architecture students the world over for a number of years. It would seem that he has succeeded in creating the long sought-for bridge between East and West, creating astonishing sanctuaries of silence and light with an intentionally limited vocabulary of geometric forms. The two projects by Ando featured in this volume, his 4 x 4 House II in Kobe and the hhstyle.com/casa building in Tokyo, are not made of concrete as it happens, but they both retain the kind of mastery of geometry and modern forms that have made Ando justifiably famous.

Born the same year as Ando, Toyo Ito may not have achieved the kind of international celebrity as the Osaka architect, but he is clearly one of the leading figures of his generation in architecture. Usually attached to extremely light designs, as opposed to the more solid concrete of Ando, Toyo Ito completed two structures recently that won him considerable media attention. One is the Médiathèque in Sendai, completed in 2001. Making use of 13 structural white steel tubes that undulate through the structure like "seaweed" to hold up the building and carry its technical conduits, Ito innovated at the most basic level of structural integrity and the aesthetics of architecture. More ephemeral, his 2002 pavilion in London's Kensington Park for the Serpentine Gallery was a 309 m² single-story structure covered in aluminum panels and glass. His concept was to create a columnless structure that is not dependent on an orthogonal grid system, making an open space to be used during the summer months as a café and event space. An algorithm derived from the rotation of a single square determined the seemingly random structure. Each piece of the structure functioned not only as a beam but also to absorb vibrations so that all elements combine to form a complex, mutually interdependent whole. The point, as explained by the architect, was "to render visible again the systems that make the most basic conditions of architecture."

RISING STARS

Toyo Ito's office has been quite effective in forming talent. One of the most famous of his former employees is Kazuyo Sejima, who worked with him between 1981 and 1987 before forming her own office. Sejima, now a partner of Ryue Nishizawa (SANAA), has leapt to international prominence with recent competition victories in Toledo (Glass Pavilion), New York (the New Museum of Contemporary Art), or Lens where she was recently selected to design the prestigious extension of the Louvre Museums. It might be said that Sejima, like her mentor, makes frequent use of impressions of extreme lightness or plays on reflection and transparency, which sometimes make it difficult to know where a building ends and where it begins. Such is the case of her Kanazawa 21st Century Museum of Contemporary Art featured here. Within a basic, simple round plan, she has created a series of galleries and a variety of experiences for the visitor that defy what one might expect of modern architecture.

Sejima's generation in Japanese architecture is particularly rich in talent. Kengo Kuma (born 1954), Shigeru Ban (born 1957), Shuhei Endo (born 1960), Jun Aoki (born 1956), and Makoto Sei Watanabe (born 1952) offer a remarkable panorama of styles and innovative architecture that would make most countries jealous. The best-known of these figures is Shigeru Ban, who has successfully introduced the idea of using paper in architecture as a structural material. At this point he is almost fully absorbed by a major French project, the new Centre Pompidou planned for the city of Metz. In an interesting play on recent architectural history, he has installed his own studio, made in part of paper on the roof of the Piano & Rogers Centre Pompidou in Paris. Ban has a gift of creating ephemeral architecture, as his unexpected Bianimale Nomadic Museum erected on Pier 54 in New York from March 5 to June 6, 2005, showed. Intended to display the work of a photographer, the 4 180m² structure was made up essentially of steel shipping containers and paper tubes made from recycled paper, with inner and outer waterproof membranes and coated with a waterproof sealant.

Kengo Kuma has worked essentially within Japan, completing the Nagasaki Prefecture Art Museum in March 2005 and the very visible One Omotesando building in Tokyo in 2003. There is a sense of humor and sophistication in Kuma's work as seen, for example, in his Great (Bamboo) Wall guest house (Beijing, 2002) that sets him apart in the contemporary architecture scene. Like Kuma, Jun Aoki has worked extensively in Japan for the French LVMH luxury group, creating stores for Louis Vuitton in New York and in Tokyo. His sense of surface effects, as seen on the corner of 57th Street and Fifth Avenue (Vuitton) or in Omotesando for the same brand, gives a life and variety to buildings that goes far beyond their association with any given type of merchandise. Shuhei Endo, like Shigeru Ban, has experimented extensively with the very forms of architecture, asking why a curving metal surface cannot form both the interior and the exterior of a house, for example. He also has worked on the idea of where a roof ends and begins (Rooftecture series). Makoto Sei Watanabe is another unusual architect, who won early fame with his controversial Aoyama Technical College (Shibuya, Tokyo, 1989) inspired by cartoon graphics. More recently he has delved extensively into computer-generated forms that can be likened to biological systems, and won commissions to design both subway and railway stations, a highly atypical event in the staid world of Japanese mass transport.

AGE OF REASON

It can be said that the "age of reason" or at least of reasonable notoriety in architecture is 40. Japanese architects are no exception, and the upcoming generation born in the early 1960s is promising indeed. The architects selected for this volume in that age group are Hitoshi Abe (born 1962) Masaki Endoh (born 1963), Makoto Yokomizo (born 1962) and Takaharu and Yui Tezuka (born 1964 and 1969). Hitoshi Abe received wide attention in the architectural press for his Reihoku Community Hall (Reihoku, Kumamoto, 2001–02), a 993 m^2 laminated dark cedar structure with an unusual billowing exterior appearance and a design intended to give the small community maximum flexibility. Masaki Endoh, working often with the engineer Masahiro Ikeda, who was born in Shizuoka in 1964, has created a series of unusual houses. He usually gives his designs the name "Natural"—as in the "Natural Wedge" featured here. He explains that this is because he believes that architecture must be based on "common sense and empirical knowledge." He goes on to say "I believe that the design process is similar to evolution. Design that incorporates new concepts will survive into the future. Design that does not change over time will disappear. It is important to constantly challenge the established norms for this architectural evolution to continue." Takaharu and Yui Tezuka certainly also believe in challenging accepted norms as their surprising Matsunoyama Natural Science Museum (Niigata, 2002-04) proves. The structure is essentially a Corten steel tube designed to resist snow loads of up to 2 000 tons that meanders over a length of 111 meters, following the topography and allowing visitors to "experience the light and colors under the different depths of snow from 4 m deep to 30 m above the ground."

Whether it be this younger generation that has yet to attain international fame, or in established figures ranging from Tadao Ando to Kazuyo Sejima, Japanese architecture has vanquished the difficulties it once faced in finding the appropriate juncture between national tradition and international modernity. As it happens, a good part of Japanese tradition, such as that exemplified at Katsura, has provided a way of approaching the link between past, present, and future that has eluded many Western architects. Accepting ambiguity, as seen in the evanescent reflections of Sejima's Kanazawa Museum, or in Makoto Yokomizo's Tomihiro Art Museum, is a key to understanding and appreciating what makes Japanese architecture different from that of Europe or America, but today ideas travel quickly. Aided by a construction industry that produces remarkable quality with materials like aluminum and concrete, Japan is a force to be reckoned with in contemporary architecture.

Philip Jodidio

EINLEITUNG

LOB DER MEHRDEUTIGKEIT

Japan ist flächenmäßig nur wenig kleiner als Kalifornien, hatte im Juli 2005 aber eine geschätzte Bevölkerungszahl von knapp 127,42 Millionen, von denen etwa zwei Millionen in den letzten zehn Jahren hinzugekommen sind. Allerdings wächst auch die Zahl der Senioren. Mit nur 0,6 % der Fläche Japans beherbergt Tokio 10 % der Einwohner des Landes, was einer extremen Bevölkerungsdichte von statistisch 5655 Personen pro Quadratkilometer entspricht. Weite Teile der Ostküste Japans zwischen Tokio und Osaka bilden ein fast ununterbrochenes städtisches Ballungsgebiet, während der bergige Westen des Landes dünner besiedelt ist. Das Wissen um diese Fakten zur Bevölkerungsdichte ist für das Verständnis der japanischen Architektur, insbesondere der Wohnarchitektur, unerlässlich. Ein weiterer wichtiger Faktor für die Architektur Japans ist die permanente Gefährdung aller Bauten durch Katastrophen. Vom Menschen verursachte Desaster und Naturkatastrophen haben nacheinander das Erscheinungsbild von Städten wie Tokio geprägt. Die erste Katastrophe im 20. Jahrhundert war das große Kanto-Erdbeben von 1923 mit einer Stärke von 7,9 auf der Richterskala, das geschätzte 200 000 Todesopfer forderte und 64% der Überlebenden obdachlos machte. Die zweite, noch verheerendere Katastrophe war der Abwurf der amerikanischen Brandbomben auf Tokio zwischen März und Mai 1945. In diesen Monaten starben mehr Menschen als an dem einen Tag, als die Atombombe auf Hiroshima fiel. Im September 1945 war die Bevölkerung Japans, die 1942 noch 6,9 Millionen stark gewesen war, durch Tod oder Emigration auf 2,777 Millionen geschrumpft. Brandbomben waren in einer Stadt wie Tokio, die hauptsächlich aus Holzhäusern bestand, besonders „effektiv". Deshalb kann man sagen, dass die größte Stadt der Welt nach 1945 praktisch vollkommen neu gebaut wurde. Anfänglich standen nur begrenzte Wiederaufbaumittel zur Verfügung. Wie im kriegszerstörten Europa war es vorrangig, schnell und preisgünstig zu bauen. In jüngerer Zeit ist das Bauen vor allem von der unerbittlichen Logik der Rentabilität bestimmt worden, die sich wenig um ästhetische Gesichtspunkte kümmerte. In gewisser Weise stellt diese Flutwelle schlechter Architektur die zweite vom Menschen verursachte Katastrophe in Tokios jüngster Geschichte dar, die viel von der Schönheit jahrhundertealter Bautraditionen vernichtet hat.

Das Aufblühen der modernen japanischen Architektur kann als sukzessive Befreiung von westlichen Einflüssen begriffen werden. Als Kommodore Matthew Perry auf seiner Expedition von 1853/54 die Stadt Edo besuchte, beschrieb er deren Landschaft als „ausgedehnte Ebene vor einer herrlichen Kulisse aus Bergen und Wäldern". Die weit reichenden Folgen der Perry-Expedition sind vielfach untersucht worden, man muss dazu aber sagen, dass die Meiji-Regierung den englischen Architekten und Stadtplaner Thomas Waters bereits 1872 damit beauftragte, die Gebäude im südöstlichen Abschnitt des Kaiserlichen Palastes wieder aufzubauen, die in jenem Jahr einem Brand zum Opfer gefallen waren. Waters schuf eine Reihe neoklassizistischer Gebäude beidseits eines breiten Boulevards, der als Ginza berühmt wurde. Ein anderer Engländer, Josiah Conder (1852–1920), baute zahlreiche massive Backsteingebäude des Zweiten Kaiserreichs – etwa das Nationalmuseum im Ueno-Park (1882) –, die zu Symbolen des japanischen Establishments wurden, bis das Kabinettsministerium beschloss, fortan die deutschen Architekten Her-

mann Ende (1829–1907) und Wilhelm Böckmann (1832–1902) zu engagieren. Ihr Entwurf für das Gebäude des Japanischen Reichstags im preußischen Stil in Pagodenform stieß auf allgemeine Ablehnung und machte deutlich, dass der Konflikt zwischen einheimischen und westlichen Architekturstilen eine Lösung erforderte.[1]

„Unter der acht Fuß dicken obersten Bodenschicht befand sich eine sechzig bis siebzig Fuß dicke, weiche Schlammschicht. Dieser Schlamm erschien wie eine gnädige Vorkehrung – ein gutes Kissen, um die furchtbaren Erschütterungen abzufangen. Warum das Gebäude nicht darauf schwimmen lassen? Ein Kriegsschiff schwimmt auf Meerwasser ..."[2] So beschreibt Frank Lloyd Wright, ein anderer ausländischer Architekt, der in Japan baute, seinen Entwurf für das Imperial Hotel in Tokio (1916–22). Dieser 1967 abgerissene exzentrische Bau überstand sogar das verheerende Erdbeben von 1923 und festigte dadurch Wrights guten Ruf, nicht zuletzt in Japan.

Wright war natürlich nicht der einzige westliche Architekt, der die Entwicklung der modernen japanischen Architektur beeinflusst hat. Le Corbusier zum Beispiel, der auch heute noch viele Architekten fasziniert, machte sich in Japan einen Namen mit Bauten wie dem Nationalmuseum für westliche Kunst im Ueno Park, Tokio (1959), und durch Arbeiten japanischer Architekten wie Kunio Maekawa, der von 1928 bis 1930 in Le Corbusiers Pariser Büro arbeitete, bevor er 1935 in Tokio sein eigenes Büro gründete. Maekawa schuf die 1979 fertig gestellte Erweiterung des genannten Museums von Le Corbusier und bestätigte damit dessen Bedeutung in und für Japan.

Am 4. November 1935 schrieb der deutsche Architekt Bruno Taut (1880–1938) in sein Tagebuch, er könne mit Fug und Recht behaupten, der Entdecker von Katsura zu sein. Er bezog sich dabei auf die kaiserliche „Villa" aus dem 17. Jahrhundert bei Kyoto, die für die Entwicklung der zeitgenössischen Architektur Japans von großer Bedeutung gewesen ist. Die Japaner hatten die nach der Perry-Expedition auf sie einströmenden westlichen Einflüsse auf unterschiedlichste Art und Weise aufgenommen und verarbeitet und sich nach und nach in vielen Aspekten von ihrer eigenen traditionellen Kultur abgewandt. Der Aufstieg des Faschismus in Japan ging daher auch einher mit einer gewissen Ablehnung der westlich inspirierten Architekturmoderne und mit der Hinwendung zum „teikan yoshiki", dem „imperialen Dachstil" mit klobigen kubischen Strukturen und ebenso klobigen „japanischen" Dächern. Taut landete im Mai 1933 in Japan und verbrachte dreieinhalb Jahre dort. Während dieser Zeit schrieb er mehrfach über die Villa Katsura, setzte ihre elegante Schlichtheit in Bezug zu den Zielen der Moderne und nannte sie ein „unvergängliches Baudenkmal". Arata Isozaki hat darauf hingewiesen, dass andere Architekten aus dem Westen wie etwa der Deutsche Gustav Pratz die Villa Katsura schon vor Taut besucht und deren Lehren in ihre „Erneuerung der Weltarchitektur"[3]

[1] „Order and Anarchy: Tokyo from 1868 to the Present," von William Coaldrake in „Tokyo, Form and Spirit", Walker Art Center, Harry N. Abrams, New York, 1986.

[2] Frank Lloyd Wright, „An Autobiography," Duell, Sloan und Pearce, New York, 1943.

[3] Arata Isozaki, „Katsura: A Model for Post-Modern Architecture," in „Katsura Villa - Space and Form," Iwanami Shoten Publishers, Tokio, 1983.

integriert hatten. Die Wiederentdeckung der grundlegenden Verwandtschaft zwischen der Reinheit der traditionellen japanischen Bauweise und der Klarheit der Moderne fand in Japan erst nach dem Trauma des Zweiten Weltkriegs statt, zum Teil weil der Rückgriff auf alte Traditionen von der nun diskreditierten herrschenden Ideologie missbraucht worden war.

MEISTER IHRER KUNST

Die nach dem Zweiten Weltkrieg einsetzende Rückbesinnung der Japaner auf ihre eigenen Traditionen wurde auch von Architektenpersönlichkeiten wie dem 1913 geborenen Kenzo Tange gefördert, der in den 1930er Jahren im Büro von Kunio Maekawa gearbeitet hatte. Tanges Sporthalle für die Olympischen Spiele in Tokio von 1964 markierte den Beginn einer japanischen Moderne, die – was Qualität und Erfindungsreichtum anging – der westlichen in nichts nachstand. Als Architekt des Friedensparks und Museums von Hiroshima, einer bewegenden Stätte des Gedenkens an die verheerenden Folgen des Atombombenabwurfs über dieser Stadt, ist Tange (gest. 2005) eine Symbolfigur der japanischen Architekturmoderne geblieben, obwohl sein Spätwerk (darunter die 1991 fertig gestellte Stadthalle von Tokio, 243 m hohe Doppeltürme, die drei Straßenblöcke im Shinjuku-Viertel einnehmen) vielen als ein Symbol für die Exzesse der Postmoderne gilt.

Einige der führenden zeitgenössischen Architekten Japans waren am Anfang ihrer Karriere Mitarbeiter von Kenzo Tange, darunter Arata Isozaki und Yoshio Taniguchi. Beide sind deshalb bedeutende Vertreter ihres Fachs geworden, weil es ihnen gelang, die Vorzüge der japanischen Architektur zu exportieren, vor allem in die USA. Isozaki gehört längst zu den sechs oder sieben japanischen „Stararchitekten", deren Bauten die Welt umspannen. Isozakis Museum of Contemporary Art in Los Angeles (1981–86) war eines der ersten Gebäude eines ausländischen Architekten in den USA, und Taniguchis Erweiterungsbau des New Yorker Museum of Modern Art beweist, dass japanische Architekten inzwischen sogar im „innersten Heiligtum" des Kunst-Establishments angekommen sind. In der Architektengeneration von Isozakis und Taniguchis genießt auch Fumihiko Maki internationales Ansehen; in den letzten Jahren hat er unter anderem ein neues Hochhaus für die Vereinten Nationen in New York und Gebäude für den Aga Khan in Kanada geplant. Wie Taniguchi hat auch Maki zum Teil in den USA studiert und spricht fließend Englisch, während die meisten bedeutenden japanischen Architekten diese Sprache noch immer nicht beherrschen. Ein weiterer vor dem Zweiten Weltkrieg geborener Meister ist Hiroshi Hara, Architekt zahlreicher prominenter Bauten in Japan – zum Beispiel des Umeda Sky Building, Kita-ku, Osaka (1988–93) und des gewaltigen JR-Bahnhofs von Kyoto (Sakyo-ku, 1990–97). Hara hat aber auch viele Einfamilienhäuser gebaut, etwa das hier vorgestellte Orimoto-Haus – stets mit demselben innovativen und intelligenten Ansatz, der sein Werk auszeichnet.

Tadao Ando ist vielleicht der weltweit bekannteste japanische Architekt der Gegenwart. Mit ihm hat sein Land auf dem Gebiet der Architektur tatsächlich den höchsten internationalen Bekanntheitsgrad erreicht. 1941 in Osaka geboren, ist Tadao Ando als Architekt Autodidakt, seine Kenntnisse und Erfahrungen erwarb er zunächst im Ausland: in den USA, in Europa und Afrika (1962–69). 1995 wurde er mit dem Pritzker-Preis ausgezeichnet, und neben seiner großen Zahl von Bauten in Japan hat er im Jahr 2000 das Gebäude der Pulitzer Foundation for the Arts in St Louis, Missouri, und 2002 das Modern Art Museum im texanischen Fort Worth fertig gestellt. Für den französischen Milliardär François Pinault entwarf er ein Museum für Gegenwartskunst in Paris; das Projekt wurde im Frühjahr 2005 leider aufgegeben. Andos eindrückliche Zeichnungen und ebenso starke Bauten, meist aus Beton, werden seit Jahren von Architekturstudenten in aller Welt nachgeahmt. Offenbar ist es ihm gelungen, die lang ersehnte Brücke zwischen Ost und West zu bauen, indem er erstaunliche, von Stille und Licht erfüllte Zufluchtsorte in einem bewusst reduzierten architektonischen Formenvokabular errichtet. Die beiden hier vorgestellten Bauten Andos – das 4 x 4 Haus Nr. II in Kobe und das hhstyle.com/casa-Geschäftshaus in Tokio, bestehen zwar nicht aus Beton, sind aber formal und gestalterisch ebenso meisterhaft wie alle Gebäude, für die Ando zu Recht berühmt geworden ist.

Zwar hat der gleichaltrige Toyo Ito nicht denselben Grad internationaler Berühmtheit erlangt wie Tadao Ando, er gehört aber dennoch zu den führenden Architekten seiner Generation. Im Gegensatz zu Andos massiven Betonbauten bevorzugt Ito für gewöhnlich eine extreme Leichtbauweise. Zwei seiner Entwürfe haben in den letzten Jahren in den Medien weithin Beachtung gefunden, zum einen die 2001 fertig gestellte Mediathek in Sendai, die von 13 konstruktiven weißen Stahlröhren wie von „Seetang" durchsetzt sind. Sie halten das Gebäude aufrecht und tragen die Haustechnik-Installationen. Hier ist Ito schon bei der Grundlage jedes Baus – dem Tragwerk – neue Wege gegangen, aber auch in der architektonischen Ästhetik. Sein Pavillon, der 2002 im Londoner Kensington Park für die Serpentine Gallery errichtet wurde – ein eingeschossiger, in Aluminiumpaneele und Glas gehüllter Bau auf 309 m^2 –, war von flüchtigerer Natur. Die Entwurfsidee bestand darin, einen stützenfreien Raum zu schaffen, der auch ohne ein orthogonales Grundrissraster auskam, einen offenen Raum, der sich im Sommer als Café und Veranstaltungsort nutzen ließ. Ein aus der Rotation eines einzigen Quadrats abgeleiteter Algorithmus bestimmte die scheinbar willkürliche Form. Jede Komponente des Pavillons hatte nicht nur eine konstruktive, sondern auch eine schwingungsdämpfende Funktion, so dass alle zusammen ein Ganzes bildeten, in dem alle Teile voneinander abhängig waren. Laut Auskunft des Architekten ging es darum, „die Systeme wieder sichtbar zu machen, welche der Architektur zugrunde liegen".

AUFGEHENDE STERNE

Toyo Itos Architekturbüro ist in der Ausbildung junger Talente ziemlich erfolgreich gewesen. Eine seiner bekanntesten ehemaligen Mitarbeiterinnen ist Kazuyo Sejima, die von 1981 bis 1987 im Büro Ito tätig war, bevor sie sich selbstständig machte. Das Büro SANAA von Sejima und Partner Ryue Nishizawa hat sich in jüngster Zeit mit siegreichen Wettbewerbsentwürfen für Toledo, Spanien (Glaspavillon), New York (New Museum of Contemporary Art) und Lens, Frankreich (Musée du Louvre), international einen Namen gemacht. Man könnte sagen, dass Sejima wie ihr Mentor Ito extreme Leichtigkeit anstrebt oder mit Spiegelungen und Transparenz spielt, so dass manchmal schwer zu sagen ist, wo ihre Bauten anfangen oder enden – so etwa beim hier vorgestellten Museum der Kunst des 21. Jahrhunderts in Kanazawa: Auf einem einfachen runden Grundriss hat sie eine Reihe von Ausstellungsräumen und „Raum-Erlebnissen" geschaffen, die alle gängigen Vorstellungen von moderner Architektur in Frage stellen.

Unter Sejimas japanischen Kollegen ihrer Generation finden sich viele Talente. Kengo Kuma (Jahrgang 1954), Shigeru Ban (1957), Shuhei Endo (1960), Jun Aoki (1956) oder Makoto Sei Watanabe (1952) etwa repräsentieren ein bemerkenswert breites Spektrum an Stilen und innovativen Bauweisen, das andere Länder vor Neid erblassen lassen könnte. Der Bekannteste unter ihnen ist Shigeru Ban, der mit großem Erfolg Papier als konstruktives Material in die Architektur eingeführt hat. Derzeit (2005/06) ist er fast ausschließlich mit der Planung des neuen Centre Pompidou für die Stadt Metz beschäftigt. In einem interessanten Spiel mit der neueren Architekturgeschichte hat er für sich ein Büro auf dem Dach des Pariser Centre Pompidou von Piano & Rogers gebaut – teilweise aus Papier. Ban besitzt besonderes Geschick für „ephemere Architektur", wie sein erstaunliches, vom 5. März bis zum 6. Juni 2005 am Pier 54 in New York aufgestelltes Nomadic Museum für die Bianimale-Stiftung gezeigt hat. Der 4180 m² große Ausstellungsraum für die Arbeiten eines Fotografen wurde im Wesentlichen aus Schiffscontainern (Stahl) und Pappröhren (Altpapier) gebaut und innen wie außen mit Folien verkleidet, die mit Dichtungsmittel wasserdicht beschichtet wurden.

Kengo Kuma hat überwiegend in Japan gebaut, unter anderem das Kunstmuseum der Präfektur Nagasaki (2005) und das weithin sichtbare Hochhaus One Omotesando in Tokio (2003). Kumas Architektur ist humorvoll und von subtiler Raffinesse, wie etwa sein „Great (Bamboo) Wall"-Gästehaus in Peking (2002) belegt, das ihn als Ausnahmeerscheinung in der heutigen Architekturszene ausweist. Auch Jun Aoki hat viel in Japan gebaut, unter anderem für die französische Unternehmensgruppe der Luxusklasse Louis Vuitton Moët Hennessy (LVMH) deren Boutique in Tokio, aber auch die in New York, 57th Street/Ecke Fifth Avenue. Beide Vuitton-Bauten belegen Aokis Sinn für Oberflächeneffekte, die ein Gebäude weit über jede Assoziation mit „verkaufsförderndem Design" beleben und abwechslungsreich gestalten. Wie Shigeru Ban hat auch Shuhei Endo mit den grundlegenden Formen der Architektur experimentiert und zum Beispiel gefragt, wieso eine gebogene Metallfläche nicht sowohl die Innenwand als auch die Außenfassade eines Hauses bilden kann. Außerdem hat er sich mit der Frage auseinandergesetzt, wo ein Dach endet bzw. anfängt (Serie der „rooftectures"). Makoto Sei Watanabe ist ein weiterer Ausnahmearchitekt, der schon früh durch sein Aoyama Technical College in Shibuya, Tokio (1989) berühmt wurde, bei dessen Gestaltung er sich von Cartoons inspirieren ließ. In jüngerer Zeit hat er sich ausgiebig mit computergestütztem Entwerfen in Anlehnung an Formen biologischer Systeme beschäftigt und Wettbewerbe für U-Bahn-Stationen und Bahnhöfe gewonnen, was in der konventionellen Welt des japanischen Massentransports vollkommen ungewöhnlich ist.

ZEITALTER DER VERNUNFT
Man könnte sagen, dass ein Architekt mit 40 Jahren sein persönliches „Zeitalter der Vernunft" oder zumindest der begründeten Bekanntheit erreicht. Japanische Architekten sind darin keine Ausnahme, und die Anfang der 1960er Jahre

Geborenen sind tatsächlich vielversprechend. Zu den für dieses Buch ausgewählten Architekten gehören daher Hitoshi Abe (Jahrgang 1962), Masaki Endoh (1963), Makoto Yokomizo (1962) sowie Takaharu und Yui Tezuka (1964 und 1969). Hitoshi Abes Dorfgemeinschaftshaus in Reihoku, Kumamoto (2001–02), ein 993 m² großes Gebäude aus dunklem Zedernschichtholz mit einer ungewöhnlichen wogenden Fassade und einer Innengliederung, die der Dorfgemeinschaft so viel flexiblen Spielraum wie möglich geben sollte, fand in den Medien große Beachtung. Masaki Endoh, der oft mit dem 1964 in Shizuoka geborenen Tragwerksplaner Masahiro Ikeda zusammenarbeitet, hat eine Reihe ungewöhnlicher Häuser gebaut. Die meisten bezeichnet er mit dem Adjektiv „natürlich" – auch das hier vorgestellte „Natural Wedge" –, weil er davon überzeugt ist, dass Architektur auf „gesundem Menschenverstand und empirischem Wissen" beruhen muss: „Für mich ähnelt der Entwurfsprozess der Evolution", sagt Endoh. „Entwürfe, die neue Konzepte enthalten, werden auch in Zukunft Bestand haben. Entwürfe, die sich nicht mit der Zeit anpassen, werden verschwinden. Es ist wichtig, die etablierten Normen ständig zu hinterfragen, wenn die architektonische Evolution weitergehen soll." Auch Takaharu und Yui Tezuka sind der Meinung, dass akzeptierte Normen in Frage gestellt werden müssen. Das belegt ihr erstaunliches Museum für Naturwissenschaften in Matsunoyama, Niigata (2002–04). Es ist im Wesentlichen eine Röhre aus Cortenstahl, die so bemessen wurde, dass sie Schneelasten von bis zu 2000 Tonnen standhält. Sie schlängelt sich in Anpassung an die Topografie über 111 m dahin und bietet Besuchern das Erlebnis „des Lichts und der Farben unter vier bis 30 Meter dicken Schneedecken".

Ob es sich um die Werke der jüngeren Generation handelt, die noch nicht international berühmt sind, oder um die Bauten weltweit anerkannter Architekten von Tadao Ando bis Kazuyo Sejima – die japanischen Architekten haben die anfänglichen Schwierigkeiten bei der Suche nach der geeigneten Verbindung zwischen nationalen Traditionen und internationaler Moderne überwunden. Vieles in den traditionellen Bauweisen Japans – exemplarisch verkörpert in der Villa Katsura – hat ihnen den Weg zu dieser Fusion von ferner Vergangenheit und Zukunft gewiesen, der so manchem westlichen Architekten versperrt geblieben ist. Die Akzeptanz von Mehrdeutigkeit, wie man sie an den flüchtigen Lichtreflexen auf Sejimas Museum in Kanazawa oder Makoto Yokomizos Tomihiro Museum ablesen kann, ist der Schlüssel zum Verständnis und zur Wertschätzung dessen, was die japanische von der europäischen oder amerikanischen Architektur unterscheidet. Allerdings verbreiten sich Ideen heutzutage mit rasender Geschwindigkeit. Unterstützt von einer Bauindustrie, die Aluminium- und Betonteile von hervorragender Qualität produziert, stellen die Japaner eine in der internationalen zeitgenössischen Architektur nicht zu unterschätzende Kraft dar.

Philip Jodidio

INTRODUCTION

HOMMAGE À L'AMBIGUÏTÉ

Légèrement moins grand que la Californie, le Japon possède une population beaucoup plus importante estimée en juillet 2005 à 127 417 244 habitants. Au cours de la dernière décennie, elle s'est accrue d'environ deux millions de personnes même si, dans les faits, le Japon vieillit. Tokyo qui est certainement la ville la plus moderne du monde représente 0,6 % de la surface du pays mais 10 % de ses habitants, soit une densité extrêmement élevée de 5655 personnes au kilomètre carré. Une grande partie de la côte est, entre Tokyo et Osaka, n'est plus pratiquement qu'une immense agglomération, tandis qu'à l'ouest subsistent encore des zones plus montagneuses et moins peuplées. Ces données, et en particulier la densité urbaine, sont importantes pour bien comprendre l'architecture japonaise en particulier dans le domaine du logement. Un autre facteur significatif est un sentiment constant de fragilité, né d'une histoire marquée par les catastrophes. Des désastres successifs, certains naturels, d'autres provoqués par l'homme, ont ainsi façonné le visage du Tokyo contemporain. Le premier du XXe siècle fut le grand tremblement de terre de Kanto en 1923 (7,9 sur l'échelle de Richter) qui a tué 200 000 Tokyoïtes et laissé 64 % de la population sans abri. Le second, plus radical encore dans ses destructions, fut les bombardements américains de mars à mai 1945. Davantage de personnes moururent au cours de ces quelques mois que lors de l'anéantissement instantané d'Hiroshima. En septembre 1945, la population qui dépassait 6,9 millions d'habitants en 1942 était tombée à 2 777 000 du fait des morts de la guerre et de l'émigration. Les bombes incendiaires lancées sur une ville essentiellement constituée de constructions en bois furent redoutablement efficaces. On peut dire que la plus grande ville du monde a été presque entièrement reconstruite depuis 1945, mais, au départ, cette reconstruction ne disposait que de moyens limités. Comme dans l'Europe ravagée de la même période, il était essentiel de construire vite et à moindre coût. Plus récemment, une implacable logique économique peu soucieuse des canons esthétiques a exercé une très forte influence. En quelque sorte, la marée de mauvaise architecture est le second désastre d'origine humaine qui a frappé l'histoire récente de la capitale. Elle a balayé une bonne part des splendeurs et des beautés léguées par des siècles de traditions.

L'émergence de l'architecture japonaise moderne peut s'analyser en termes de libération progressive des influences occidentales. Lorsque le commodore Perry découvre la ville d'Edo au cours de son expédition de 1853-1854, il parle d'« une vaste plaine sur un magnifique fond de montagnes et de paysages boisés ». Les lointaines conséquences de cette expédition ont souvent été étudiées, mais il faut rappeler que, dès 1872, le gouvernement Meiji fit appel à l'architecte et urbaniste britannique Thomas Waters pour reconstruire le secteur au sud-est du Palais impérial détruit par un incendie. Le long d'une large avenue qui allait devenir Ginza, Waters dessina des bâtiments néoclassiques. Un autre Anglais, Josiah Conder (1852-1920) édifia de nombreux bâtiments pesants de style Second Empire, comme le Musée national du Parc d'Uneo (1882), qui devinrent les symboles de l'establishment japonais jusqu'à ce que le Ministère du Cabinet décide de faire appel aux Allemands Hermann Ende (1829-1907) et Wilhelm Böckmann (1832-1902). Leur plan de style prussien pour la Diète japonaise et sa toiture surmontée d'une sorte de pagode soulevèrent une opposition concertée et provoqua des appels à la résolution du conflit entre les styles architecturaux locaux et occidentaux.[1]

« Il y avait de soixante à soixante-dix pieds de boue liquide sous huit pieds de terre. Cette boue semblait un don du ciel, un coussin efficace pour amortir les terribles chocs. Pourquoi ne pas laisser le bâtiment flotter au-dessus ? Un bateau de guerre flotte bien sur l'eau salée ... »[2] C'est ainsi qu'un autre architecte étranger, Frank Lloyd Wright, décrit ses plans pour l'Imperial Hotel de Tokyo (1916–22). Démolie en 1967, cette construction excentrique était célèbre pour avoir résisté au séisme de 1923, ce qui avait conforté la réputation du maître, en particulier au Japon.

Bien sûr, Wright n'a pas été le seul Occidental a exercer une influence sur le développement de l'architecture moderne japonaise. Le Corbusier, par exemple, qui fascine encore de nombreux architectes contemporains, fut également présent à travers des projets comme le Musée national d'art occidental du Parc d'Ueno à Tokyo (1959) et ceux de certains de ses élèves comme Kunio Maekawa qui avait travaillé dans son atelier parisien de 1928 à 1930 avant d'ouvrir sa propre agence à Tokyo en 1935. Maekawa réalisa d'ailleurs en 1979 l'extension de ce même musée, réaffirmant symboliquement l'importance de Le Corbusier dans son pays.

Le 4 novembre 1935, l'architecte allemand Bruno Taut (1880-1938) écrivait dans son journal : « Je peux vraiment prétendre avoir découvert Katsura. » Cette affirmation sur cette résidence impériale du XVIIe siècle proche de Kyoto est d'une importance considérable pour l'évolution de l'architecture contemporaine japonaise. Alors que le Japon, à de nombreux égards, assimilait les influences occidentales auxquelles il était exposé depuis l'expédition Perry, il en était venu à rejeter de nombreux aspects de ses propres traditions. Ainsi la montée du fascisme au Japon s'est accompagnée d'un certain rejet d'une modernité d'inspiration occidentale en faveur d'une architecture appelée « teikan yoshiki » ou « style des toits impériaux » qui produisit de lourds bâtiments surmontés de toits « japonais » tout aussi disgracieux. Arrivé au Japon en mai 1933, Taut y séjourna trois ans et demi pour écrire sur Katsura. Il fit un lien entre la simplicité élégante de la villa et les objectifs du mouvement moderne et la qualifia de « monument éternel ». Comme le fait remarquer Arata Isozaki, d'autres architectes occidentaux, comme l'Allemand Gustav Prattz, avaient déjà visité Katsura, même avant Taut, et intégré ses leçons au bénéfice du « renouveau de l'architecture monoiale ».[3] La redécouverte de liens fondamentaux entre la pureté de la tradition nippone et le modernisme ne se produisit cependant qu'après le traumatisme de la Seconde Guerre mondiale, en partie parce qu'une idéologie politique fortement discréditée s'était auparavant appropriée l'idée même de s'appuyer sur la tradition.

[1] « Order and Anarchy: Tokyo from 1868 o the Present », par William Coaldrake dans « Tokyo, Form and Spirit », Walker Art Center, Harry N. Abrams, New York, 1986.

[2] Frank Lloyd Wright, « An Autobiography », Duell, Sloan et Pearce, New York, 1943.

[3] Arata Isozaki, « Katsura: A Model for Post-Modern Architecture », dans « Katsura Villa – Space and Form, » Iwanami Shoten Publishers, Tokyo, 1983.

MAÎTRES DE LEUR ART

La découverte, après la guerre, de la tradition japonaise par les Japonais eux-mêmes fut aidée par de grandes figures comme l'architecte Kenzo Tange. Né en 1913, il avait travaillé dans les années 1930 dans l'agence de Kunio Maekawa, mais ses halls pour les Jeux olympiques de Tokyo en 1964 annonçaient l'émergence d'une modernité locale comparable, en termes de qualité et d'inventivité, à celle de l'Ouest. Auteur du Parc et Musée de la paix d'Hiroshima, qui est un témoignage bouleversant de l'horreur de la bombe atomique, Tange (mort en 2005) reste un des symboles de l'architecture moderne japonaise jusqu'à ses dernières œuvres dont l'Hôtel de ville de Tokyo (1991). Ces tours jumelles de 243 m de haut qui occupent trois blocs du quartier de Shinjuku sont aussi considérées par certains comme un symbole des excès des années de la bulle spéculative.

Plusieurs figures marquantes de l'architecture contemporaine sont issues de l'agence de Kenzo Tange, en particulier Arata Isozaki et Yoshio Taniguchi. Entre autres raisons, l'importance de ces deux « élèves » vient de ce qu'ils ont réussi à faire connaître avec succès l'architecture japonaise à l'étranger, en particulier aux États-Unis. Isozaki a longtemps été l'une de ces six ou sept « stars » internationales qui parsèment le monde de leurs projets. Son Musée d'art contemporain à Los Angeles (1981–86) fut ainsi l'une des premières institutions confiées à un intervenant étranger aux États-Unis, et le récent MoMA de Taniguchi à New York montre que les Japonais ont su se faire accepter jusque dans le saint des saints même de l'establishment artistique. De la même génération, Fumihiko Maki est lui aussi très connu à l'étranger. Parmi ses récents projets figurent une nouvelle tour pour les Nations Unies à New York et des réalisations pour l'Aga Khan au Canada. Comme Taniguchi, il a été en partie formé aux États-Unis et maîtrise parfaitement l'anglais, ce qui n'est pas encore le cas de tous les grands architectes japonais. Autre maître, né avant la guerre, Hiroshi Hara est l'auteur de très nombreuses réalisations de forte visibilité comme l'immeuble Umeda Sky (Kita-ku, Osaka, 1988–93) ou la massive gare ferroviaire de JR (Akyo-ku, Kyoto, 1990–97). Il a également construit de nombreuses résidences privées dont la maison Orimoto publiée ici, toujours dans cette approche à la fois intelligente et novatrice qui caractérise son œuvre.

Tadao Ando est peut-être l'un des plus célèbres architectes du monde et c'est grâce à lui que le Japon a accédé au sommet de la notoriété internationale dans ce domaine. Né à Osaka en 1941, il est autodidacte dans le domaine de l'architecture, mais s'est en grande partie formé lors de voyages aux États-Unis, en Europe et en Afrique (1962–69). Il a reçu le Pritzker Prize en 1995 et, en dehors de ses merveilleuses réalisations japonaises, il vient d'achever le Modern Art Museum de Fort Worth (1999–2002) et la Pulitzer Foundation for the Arts (St Louis, Missouri, 1997–2000). Le projet de musée d'art contemporain pour le milliardaire français François Pinault a malheureusement été annulé au printemps 2005. La puissance de son style, qu'illustrent ses dessins et ses constructions généralement en béton, a été admirée et imitée par des étudiants du monde entier depuis de nombreuses années. Il semble qu'à travers ses étonnants sanctuaires de silence et de lumière il ait réussi à créer cette passerelle longtemps souhaitée entre l'Orient et l'Occident dans le cadre d'un vocabulaire volontairement restreint de formes géométriques. Les deux projets publiés ici, la maison appelée 4 x 4 House II à Kobé et la hhsty-

le.com/casa à Tokyo ne sont pas, pour une fois, en béton mais conservent la maîtrise géométrique et ces formes modernes qui ont rendu Ando à juste titre si célèbre.

Né la même année que Ando, Toyo Ito n'a peut-être pas encore atteint le même niveau de reconnaissance internationale que l'architecte d'Osaka, mais il est certainement l'une des figures marquantes de sa génération. Connu pour son goût pour la légèreté – par opposition aux massives structures en béton de Ando – il vient d'achever deux chantiers qui ont attiré l'attention des médias. L'un est celui de la médiathèque de Sendai, terminée en 2001. À l'aide de treize tubes d'acier structurel blanc qui ondulent comme des « algues » pour soutenir le bâtiment et acheminer les flux techniques, il fait œuvre de novateur au niveau le plus basique de l'intégrité structurelle et de l'esthétique architecturale. L'autre, plus éphémère, est son pavillon de 2002 pour la Serpentine Gallery dans le Parc de Kensington à Londres. Il s'agissait d'une petite construction de 309 m², recouverte de panneaux d'aluminium et de verre, qui servit pendant quelques mois de café et d'espace de réception. Le concept était ici de créer une structure sans colonne ni trame orthogonale. Un algorithme dérivé de la rotation d'un carré a permis de dessiner la structure. Chaque élément fonctionnait à la fois comme poutre et amortisseur de vibrations, l'ensemble formant un système complexe et totalement interdépendant. L'objectif, pour Toyo Ito, était de « rendre de nouveau visible les systèmes qui constituent les conditions les plus basiques de l'architecture ».

ÉTOILES MONTANTES

L'agence de Toyo Ito a joué un assez grand rôle dans la formation de nouveaux talents. L'une de ses anciennes collaboratrices les plus célèbres est Kazuyo Sejima, qui y avait travaillé de 1981 à 1987 avant d'ouvrir sa propre agence. Aujourd'hui associée à Ryue Nishizawa (SANAA), elle a accédé à la notoriété internationale grâce à ses victoires à des concours dont celui de Tolède (Pavillon de verre) et de New York (New Museum of Contemporary Art) qu'elle a remportés, ou celui organisé pour le projet du Louvre à Lens. Comme son mentor, elle utilise fréquemment des impressions de légèreté extrême ou des jeux de reflets ou de transparence qui font que l'on ne sait pas toujours où commence et où finit le bâtiment. C'est le cas du Musée du XXIe siècle publié ici. À l'intérieur d'un plan circulaire simple, elle a créé une série de galeries et de modes de découverte par le visiteur qui vont bien au-delà de ce que l'on pouvait attendre.

La génération de Sejima est particulièrement riche en talents nouveaux. Kengo Kuma (né en 1954), Shigeru Ban (1957), Shuhei Endo (1960), Juan Aoki (1956), ou Makoto Sei Watanabe (1952), offrent un remarquable panorama de styles et d'innovations architecturales qui pourrait rendre jaloux bien des pays. Le plus célèbre d'entre eux est Shigeru Ban, qui a introduit l'utilisation du carton en tant que matériau structurel en architecture. Actuellement, il se consacre presque exclusivement à un grand projet français, le nouveau Centre Pompidou de Metz. Petit jeu sur l'histoire de l'architecture, il a installé son propre studio, en grande partie en carton, sur le toit du Centre Pompidou de Piano et Rogers. Il possède un don pour les architectures éphémères, comme l'a montré une fois encore son très étonnant Nomadic Museum édifié en 2005 sur le Pier 54 à New York. Cette structure destinée à abriter une exposition de photographies de 4180 m² est essentiellement constituée de conteneurs maritimes et de tubes en carton faits de papier recyclé et recouverts de membranes internes et externes étanches.

Kengo Kuma a essentiellement travaillé au Japon. Après son immeuble très remarqué One Omotesando à Tokyo, il vient d'achever le Musée d'art de la préfecture de Nagasaki. Son œuvre ne manque pas d'imagination, comme le prouve, par exemple, sa « maison d'hôtes de la Grande muraille (de bambou) » (Pékin, 2002), ce qui lui confère une place à part sur la scène japonaise. Comme Kuma, Jun Aoki a beaucoup travaillé au Japon, en particulier pour le groupe de produits de luxe LVMH pour lequel il a créé des magasins Louis Vuitton à Tokyo (et aussi à New York). Son sens des effets de surface, comme on le voit dans ces deux magasins confère à ses créations une vie et une variété qui vont bien au-delà de leurs liens avec les produits de luxe. Shuhei Endo, comme Shigeru Ban, travaille sur la forme architecturale en se demandant, par exemple, pourquoi une feuille de métal incurvée ne pourrait constituer en même temps l'intérieur et l'extérieur d'une maison. Il a également réfléchi à la manière dont un toit commence et se termine (série des Rooftectures). Makoto Sei Watanabe est un autre de ces étonnants architectes. Il s'est fait très tôt connaître pour son très controversé collège technique d'Aoyama (Shibuya, Tokyo, 1989) inspiré de l'esthétique de la bande dessinée. Plus récemment, il s'est consacré à des formes générées par ordinateur, comparables à des systèmes biologiques, et a remporté des commandes pour des gares de métro et de chemin de fer, événement hautement atypique dans le monde figé des transports de masse japonais.

ÂGE DE RAISON

On peut dire que « l'âge de raison » ou, du moins, celui auquel on peut espérer atteindre à une notoriété raisonnable est, en architecture, de 40 ans. Les architectes japonais n'y font pas exception et la génération montante, née au début des années 1960 s'annonce très prometteuse. Les praticiens sélectionnés pour cet ouvrage dans ce groupe d'âge sont Hitoshi Abe (né en 1962), Masaki Endoh (1963), Makoto Yokomizo (1962) et Takaharu et Yui Tezuka (né en 1964 et 1969). Hitoshi Abe s'est fait remarquer de la presse architecturale par son Centre communautaire de Reihoku (Reihoku, Kumamoto, 2001–02), construction de 993 m² en cèdre foncé lamellé-collé dont l'aspect extérieur en forme de vague est conçu pour donner à cet équipement public le maximum de souplesse. Masaki Endoh, qui travaille souvent avec l'ingénieur Masahiro Ikeda (né en 1964) a créé toute une série de maisons surprenantes. Il donne généralement à ses projets le nom de « Naturel », comme dans « Natural Wedge » présenté ici, parce qu'il pense que l'architecture est d'appuyer sur « un sens commun et une connaissance empirique … Je crois que le processus de conception est semblable à celui de l'évolution. Un projet qui intègre de nouveaux concepts survivra dans le futur. La conception qui ne change pas avec le temps disparaîtra. Il est important de remettre constamment en question les normes établies pour que l'évolution architecturale se poursuive ». Takaharu et Yui Tezuka croient, eux aussi, à la remise en cause des normes comme l'illustre leur étonnant Musée des sciences de la nature de Matsunoyama (Nigita, 2002-04). Il

s'agit essentiellement d'un tube en acier Corten conçu pour résister à la charge de la neige qui peut atteindre 2000 tonnes. Il se fraie son chemin sur 111 mètres en suivant la topographie pour permettre aux visiteurs « d'expérimenter la lumière et les couleurs sous différentes profondeurs de neige, de 4m de profondeur à 30 m au-dessus du sol ».

Que ce soit à travers cette nouvelle génération qui attend encore une reconnaissance internationale ou ses célébrités – de Tadao Ando à Kazugo Sejima –, l'architecture japonaise a surmonté les difficultés auxquelles elle a dû faire face pour relier la tradition nationale et la modernité internationale. En fait, c'est sa tradition, illustrée par exemple par Katsura, qui lui a apporté une manière d'envisager un lien entre le passé, le présent et le futur, ce qui a échappé à beaucoup d'Occidentaux. Accepter l'ambiguïté, comme dans les reflets évanescents du Musée de Kanazawa par Sejima ou le Musée de Tomihiro par Makoto Yokomizo, est une des clés de la compréhension et de l'appréciation de la différence de cette architecture par rapport à celle de l'Europe ou de l'Amérique. Mais, aujourd'hui, les idées voyagent rapidement. Aidés par une industrie du bâtiment qui a atteint un niveau de qualité remarquable dans la construction en aluminium et en béton, les Japonais sont une force qui compte en architecture contemporaine.

Philip Jodidio

HITOSHI ABE

ATELIER HITOSHI ABE
3-3-16, Oroshimachi
Wakabayashi-ku
Sendai, Miyagi 984-0015

Tel: + 81 22 78 43 411
Fax: + 81 22 78 21 233
e-mail: house@a-slash.jp
Web: www.a-slash.jp

HITOSHI ABE was born in 1962 in Sendai, Miyagi. He worked from 1988 to 1992 in the office of Coop Himmelb(l)au and obtained his Master of Architecture degree from the Southern California Institute of Architecture (SCI-Arc) in 1989. He created his own firm, Atelier Hitoshi Abe, in 1992. From 1994, he directed the Hitoshi Abe Architectural Design Laboratory at the Tohoku Institute of Technology. He has been a Professor at Tohoku University since 2002. His work includes: the Miyagi Water Tower, Rifu, Miyagi (1994); the Gravel-2 House, Sendai, (1998); the Neige Lune Fleur Restaurant, Sendai (1999); the Miyagi Stadium, Rifu, Miyagi (2000); the Michinoku Folklore Museum, Kurikoma, Miyagi (2000); and the A-House, Sendai (2000). More recently, he has been working on the JB House, the S-Orthopedics Factory and Office Building, all located in Sendai. He won the 2003 Architectural Institute of Japan Award for the Reihoku Community Hall, Reihoku, Kumamoto (2001-02).

AOBA-TEI RESTAURANT
SENDAI
2004 - 05

FLOOR AREA: 219 m^2
CLIENT: Aoba-tei
COST: not disclosed

In this unusual two-story project, Hitoshi Abe used shipbuilding technology to manufacture the thin steel plates that were then welded in place by craftsmen who "freely deformed them by heating or chilling the surfaces, creating complex curved surfaces." As the architect explains, "By inserting an inner wall made of steel plates within a French restaurant that faces Jozenji street in Sendai city, we were attempting to design a soft boundary surface that spatially mediates between the first and second floors of the existing building, and links the inner space of the restaurant with the space defined by the famous roadside zelkova trees that symbolize Sendai." The surprising steel shell, inserted into a more rectilinear Modernist building, creates something of a cave-like atmosphere where the shapes of trees are omnipresent. Designed between December 2003 and March 2004, the Aoba-tei Restaurant was built between August 2004 and February 2005. The area of the first floor reception space is 64 m^2. A concrete floor with epoxy resin finish and steel plates with aqua urethane spray are used in this space. The dining space on the second floor measures 155 m^2 and has walnut floors and the same steel plate wall and ceiling as the entrance.

Für diesen ungewöhnlichen zweigeschossigen Bau griff Hitoshi Abe auf Techniken aus dem Schiffbau zurück, um dünne Stahlplatten herzustellen, die dann vor Ort von Fachleuten „unter Hitze- oder Kälteeinwirkung verformt wurden, um mehrfach geschwungene Oberflächen zu erhalten," und anschließend zusammengeschweißt wurden. Dazu der Architekt: „Mit dem Einsatz einer Innenwand aus Stahlplatten in dem französischen Restaurant in der Jozenji-Straße in Sendai beabsichtigten wir, eine sanfte Begrenzung zu schaffen, die räumlich zwischen dem Erdgeschoss und dem Obergeschoss des Altbaus vermittelt und den Innenraum des Restaurants mit dem Straßenraum im Schatten der berühmten Zelkova-Bäume, dem Wahrzeichen von Sendai, verbindet." Der ungewöhnliche

konvexe und konkave Stahlkörper in einem rechtwinkligen modernen Gebäude schafft ein höhlenartiges Ambiente, in dem die Bäume allgegenwärtig sind. Die Entwurfsphase dauerte von Dezember 2003 bis März 2004, die Bauzeit von August 2004 bis Februar 2005. Die Eingangshalle mit Empfang im Erdgeschoss ist 64 m^2 groß und hat einen mit Epoxidharz beschichteten Betonfußboden sowie Wände aus mit Urethan klarlackierten Stahlplatten. Der Restaurantbereich im Obergeschoss ist 155 m^2 groß; er hat einen Nussbaumboden und seine Wände und die Decke sind mit den gleichen Stahlplatten verkleidet wie die Eingangshalle.

Dans cet étonnant projet de restaurant à deux étages, Hitoshi Abe a eu recours à une technologie issue de la construction navale pour faire fabriquer de minces plaques d'acier soudées directement en place par des artisans qui « les déformèrent librement en chauffant ou réfrigérant leur surface pour en créer une différente à courbes complexes ». Comme l'explique l'architecte : « En insérant ce mur intérieur en plaques d'acier dans ce restaurant français donnant sur la rue Jozenji à Sendai, nous avons tenté de créer une frontière non agressive qui crée une jonction spatiale entre le rez-de-chaussée et l'étage tout en reliant le volume intérieur du restaurant à celui défini par les célèbres zelkovas des trottoirs de Sendai qui symbolisent la ville. » Cette surprenante coque d'acier insérée dans un bâtiment moderniste rectiligne fait naître une sorte d'atmosphère caverneuse marquée par la forme omniprésente des arbres. Conçu entre décembre 2003 et mars 2004, ce restaurant a été réalisé d'août 2004 à février 2005. La zone de réception du rez-de-chaussée, au sol en béton recouvert de résine épovy et aux murs habillés de plaques d'acier à projection d'uréthane aqueux, mesure 64 m^2. La salle à manger de l'étage, de 155 m^2, a reçu un sol en noyer et la même peau en acier tendue sur les murs et les plafonds qu'à l'entrée.

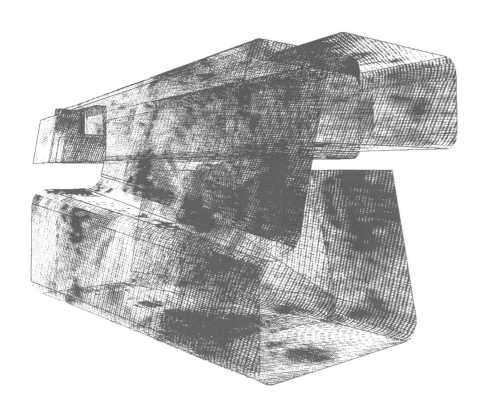

The second-floor dining area has oil-finished walnut floors, while the walls and ceilings are made with steel plate finished with aqua urethane spray. The drawing to the left shows the wrapping shell design of the interior space.

Der Restaurantbereich im Obergeschoss hat einen geölten Nussbaumboden; die Wände und Decken bestehen aus Stahlplatten, die mit Aqua-Urethan beschichtet wurden. Die Zeichnung (links) veranschaulicht die „Umhüllung" des Innenraums.

La salle à manger de l'étage possède des sols en noyer huilé et des murs et plafonds en acier traité par projection d'uréthane aqueux. À gauche, dessin montrant la coque enveloppante qui constitue l'espace intérieur.

Welded in place by skilled craftsmen, the
steel surfaces of the restaurant interior evoke
the locally prominent zelkova tree, while
providing a flowing, varied décor.

Die fachmännisch verschweißten Stahlwände
im Restaurant sind eine Reminiszenz an die
lokalen Zelkova-Bäume und erzeugen ein
abwechslungsreiches, fließendes Dekor.

Soudé sur place par des artisans de haute
compétence, les parois en acier de l'intérieur
du restaurant évoquent dans un décor animé
l'arbre local, le zelkova.

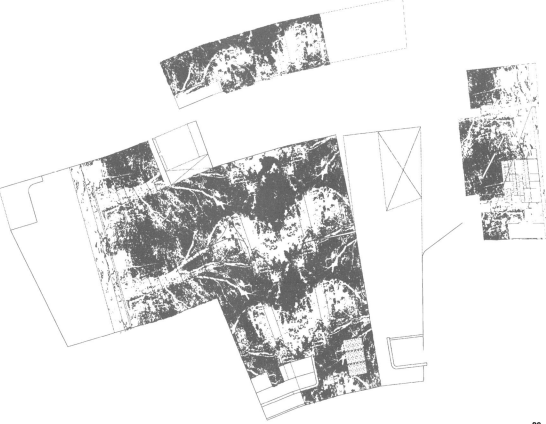

Walking up the steps from the ground floor reception area to the actual restaurant, the visitor is immediately plunged into the forest atmosphere imagined by the architect. Plans to the right show that although the steel walls give an impression of irregular space, the actual dining area is relatively simple divided between small tables and the bar with extra seating.

Wenn Gäste die Stufen vom Empfang im Erdgeschoss zum eigentlichen Restaurant heraufsteigen, tauchen sie – wie vom Architekten beabsichtigt – in ein waldähnliches Ambiente ein. Die Grundrisse (rechts) belegen, dass durch die Stahlwände zwar der Eindruck eines unregelmäßig geschnittenen Raums entsteht, der Restaurantbereich aber durch kleine Tische und eine Bar mit zusätzlichen Sitzgelegenheiten relativ einfach aufgeteilt ist.

En montant de la réception vers la salle de restaurant, l'hôte se sent absorbé par l'atmosphère de forêt imaginée par l'architecte. À droite, les plans montrent que, même si les murs d'acier créent une impression de volume irrégulier, l'aménagement de la salle reste relativement simple, partagé entre une zone de petites tables et le bar et ses sièges.

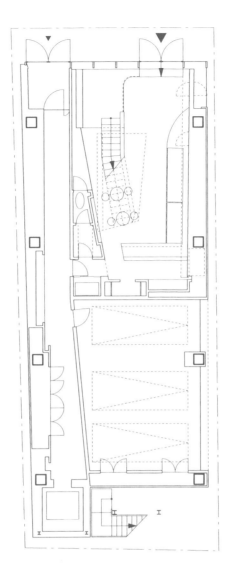
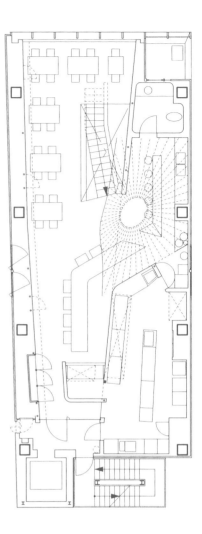

2

TADAO ANDO

TADAO ANDO ARCHITECT &
ASSOCIATES

Born in Osaka in 1941, **TADAO ANDO** was self-educated as an architect, largely through his travels in the United States, Europe and Africa (1962–69). He founded Tadao Ando Architect & Associates in Osaka in 1969. He has received the Alvar Aalto Medal, Finnish Association of Architects (1985); Medaille d'or, French Academy of Architecture (1989); the 1992 Carlsberg Prize, and the 1995 Pritzker Prize. He has taught at Yale (1987), Columbia (1988), and Harvard (1990) universities. Notable buildings include: Rokko Housing, Kobe (1983–93); the Church on the Water, Hokkaido (1988); the Japan Pavilion Expo '92, Seville, Spain (1992); the Forest of Tombs Museum, Kumamoto (1992); and the Suntory Museum, Osaka (1994). Recent work includes: the Awaji Yumebutai, Awajishima, Hyogo (1997–2000); the Modern Art Museum of Fort Worth, Fort Worth, Texas (1999–2002); and the Pulitzer Foundation for the Arts, St Louis, Missouri (1997–2000). He completed the new Chichu Art Museum on the Island of Naoshima in the Inland Sea, part of the continuing project that led him to create the Benesse House museum and hotel there beginning in the early 1990s. He won the competition to design the Pinault Foundation on the Île Seguin, Paris, but the project was canceled in 2005.

4 X 4 HOUSE II
KOBE
2004

FLOOR AREA: 84 m^2
CLIENT: Private client
COST: not disclosed

It was in 2003 that Tadao Ando completed a powerful and yet extremely simple concrete house on a beachfront site measuring just 65 m^2. Significantly for Tadao Ando, the house is only four kilometers from the Awaji Island epicenter of the 1995 Great Hanshin Earthquake that devastated Kobe. As the architect says, "The landscape framed within this cube is a panorama sweeping over the Inland Sea, the Awaji Island and the Akashi Kaikyo Bridge, where thoughts and memories of the earthquake are embedded, for both the client as well as for myself." At that time he explained, "an extension of the building on the beach in front is currently under consideration. I am dreaming of an architecture that would soak in seawater at high tide." The second house, called the 4 x 4 House II, was finished in late 2004. Ando says, "After the completion of the original '4 x 4 House,' another client came and asked me to design one for him. I suggested that the house be built on an adjacent lot but be constructed of wood." With a site area of 74 m^2, a footprint of just 23 m^2 and a total floor area of 84 m^2, the new residence is as small as its predecessor with good reason, because it is essentially a mirror image of the concrete building. Made with laminated Oregon pine, it has paulownia wood floors. Ando concludes, "By creating a pair of structures resembling a gate opening out toward the sea but built in contrasting materials, that is, in concrete and wood, I hope to reinforce the connection of the architecture to the place."

2003 baute Tadao Ando ein schlichtes, aber darum umso eindrucksvolleres Strandhaus aus Beton auf einem nur 65 m^2 großen Grundstück. Für ihn war von Bedeutung, dass es nur rund 65 km vom Epizentrum des großen Hanshin-Awaji-Erdbebens auf der Insel Awaji entfernt liegt, das auch die Stadt Kobe verwüstete. Ando erklärte dazu: „Die von diesem Kubus gerahmte Landschaft ist ein Panorama, das sich über das Binnenmeer bis zur Insel Awaji mit der Akashi Kaikyo-Brücke erstreckt, die für den Bauherrn und für mich untrennbar mit den Erinnerungen an das Erdbeben verbunden sind." Damals sei bereits ein Anbau an das Strandhaus geplant gewesen, und er habe von einem Bau geträumt, der bei Flut im Meer schwimmen könnte. Das Haus 4 x 4 Nr. II wurde Ende 2004 fertig gestellt. Dazu

erläuterte der Architekt: „Nach Fertigstellung des ersten 4 x 4-Hauses kam ein anderer Bauherr und wünschte sich ebenfalls ein Haus von mir. Ich schlug ihm vor, es auf einem benachbarten Grundstück zu errichten, aber aus Holz." Diese Parzelle misst 74 m^2, die Grundfläche des Hauses beträgt nur 23 m^2, die Gesamtfläche 84 m^2. Damit ist es ebenso klein wie der Vorläuferbau – aus gutem Grund, denn es ist im Wesentlichen ein Spiegelbild des Betonhauses. Es besteht aus Oregon-Pinien-schichtholz und hat Fußböden aus Paulownia-Holz. Ando meinte: „Indem ich ein Gebäude-Paar schuf, das sich wie ein Tor zum Meer hin öffnet, dessen Pfeiler aber aus gegensätzlichen Materialien bestehen - Beton und Holz –, wollte ich die Verbindung zwischen Architektur und Standort hervorheben."

C'est en 2003 que Tadao Ando a achevé cette maison en béton, d'une présence simple et forte, sur un terrain en front de mer d'à peine 65 m2. Il n'est pas sans importance pour l'architecte que ce site ne se trouve qu'à quatre kilomètres de l'épicentre du Grand grand tremblement de terre d'Hanshin sur l'Ile l'île d'Awaji (1995) qui dévasta Kobe. Comme il l'explique : « Le paysage cadré de l'intérieur du cube se présente sous forme d'un panorama de la Mer intérieure, de l'île d'Awaji et du pont d'Akashi Kaikyo où subsistent tant de souvenirs de ce tremblement de terre, et ceci, aussi bien pour mon client que moi-même. En ce moment, poursuit-il, « une extension de la maison sur la plage est en cours d'étude. Je rêve d'une architecture qui baignerait dans l'eau à marée haute ». La seconde maison, appelée 4 x 4 House II a été terminée fin 2004. « Après l'achèvement de la 4 x 4 House originale, un autre client m'a demandé de lui en construire une. J'ai proposé de l'édifier en bois cette fois, sur une parcelle adjacente. » Pour un terrain de 74 m^2, une emprise au sol de 23 m^2 et une surface totale de 84 m^2 la nouvelle résidence est aussi petite que la précédente dont elle est quasiment l'image réfléchie. Montée en pin d'Orégon lamifié collé, ses portes sont en paulownia. Ando ajoute : « En créant ce couple de constructions qui font penser à une porte s'ouvrant vers la mer mais réalisées en matériaux contrastés... j'espère renforcer le lien de l'architecture avec le lieu. »

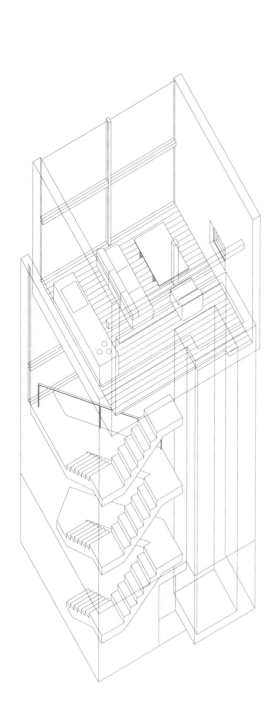

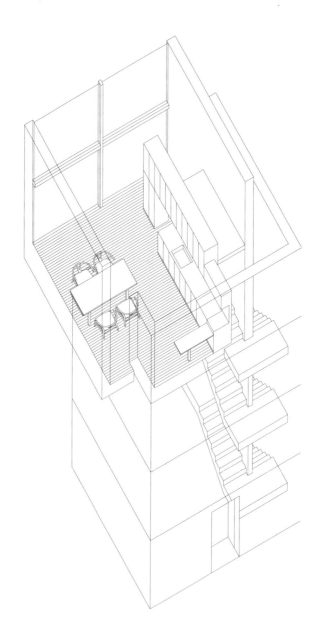

The 4 x 4 House II (right, above) is a mirror image of the original concrete 4 x 4 House, but it is made entirely of wood. Despite their limited floor areas, the two houses are spectacular and complementary.

Das 4 x 4-Haus II (rechts oben) ist ein Spiegelbild des ersten 4 x 4-Hauses aus Beton, besteht aber ganz aus Holz. Trotz ihrer kleinen Wohnfläche sind die beiden Häuser äußerst eindrucksvoll und ergänzen sich gegenseitig.

La 4 x 4House II (ci-dessus, à droite), entièrement construite en bois, est une image en miroir de la 4 x 4 d'origine en béton. De surface très réduite, les deux maisons sont spectaculaires et complémentaires.

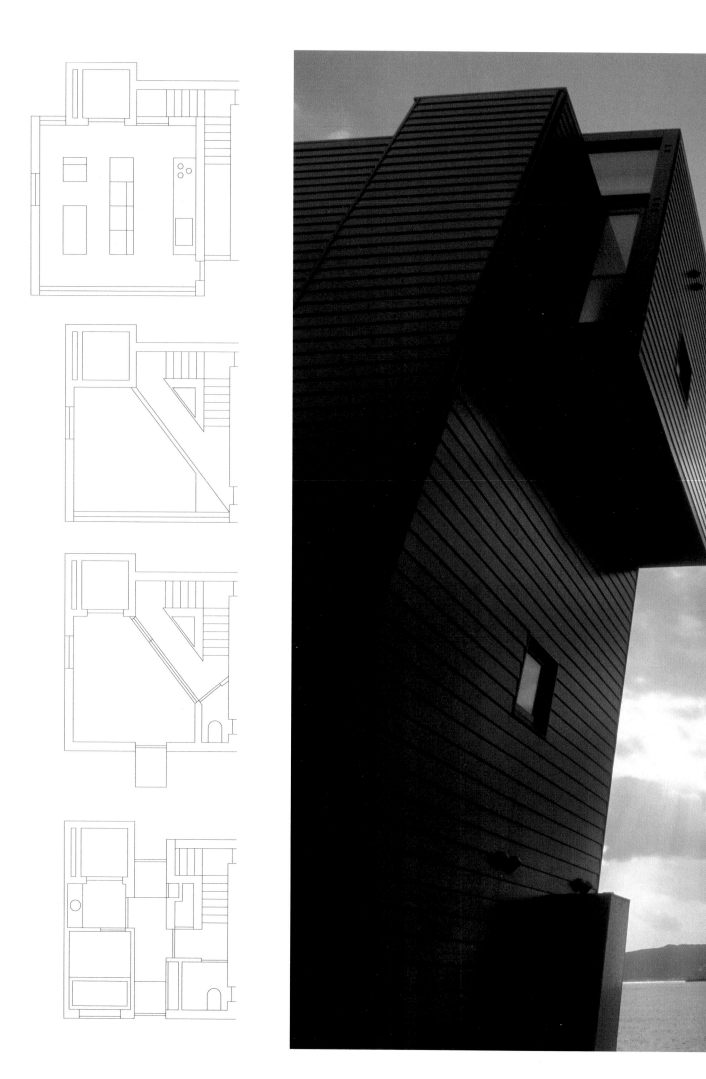

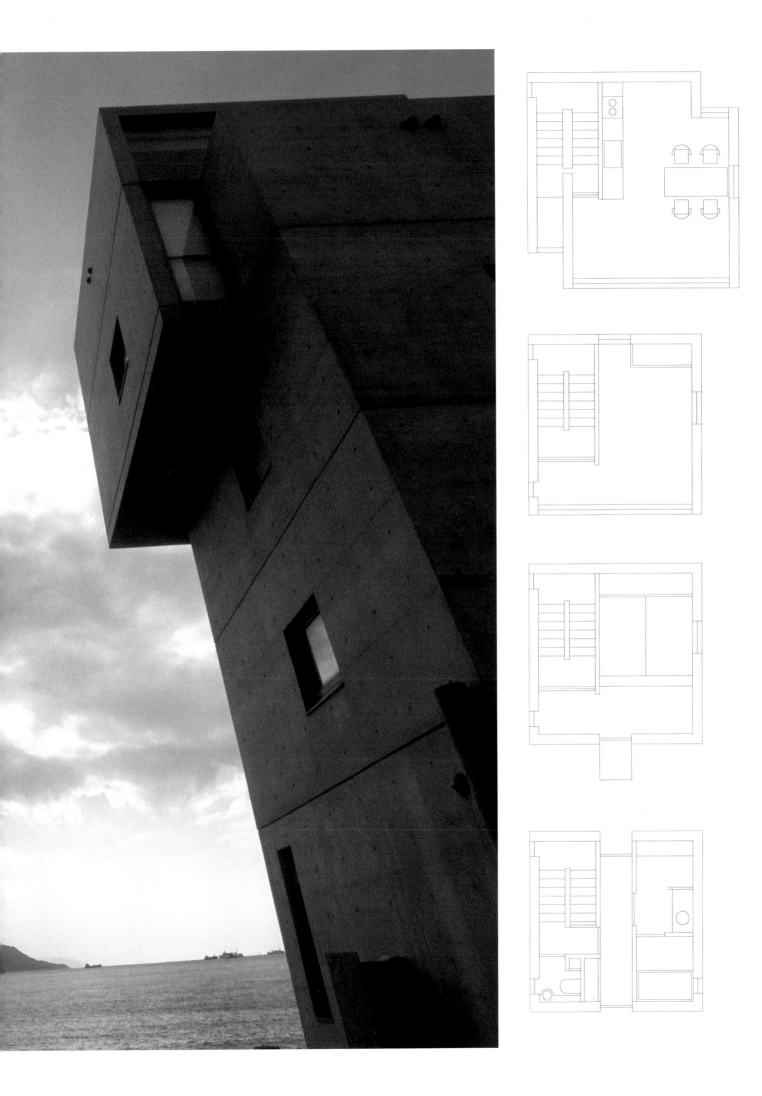

HHSTYLE.COM/CASA
TOKYO
2004-05

FLOOR AREA: 469 m^2
CLIENT: inter.office ltd.
COST: not disclosed

The stretch between Omotesando and Harajuku in Tokyo may be one of the most architecturally interesting areas in the world at present. Herzog & de Meuron (Prada), Kengo Kuma (LVMH), Toyo Ito (Tod's), and Kazuyo Sejima (Dior) have all built there. Although he has a bigger project in the works nearby, Ando's latest contribution to the district is an unusual origami-like structure fashioned from 16-mm steel plates. Although the site is relatively ample by Tokyo standards (352 m^2), part of the area is limited to steel-frame or wood construction not exceeding two stories. Furthermore, the lease for the site covers two areas, one for a ten-year period, and one for half that duration. The architect thus was called upon to concentrate most of the building on the ten-year plot. Two stories plus a basement arranged as a continuous interior space, this design store has a total floor area of 469 m^2 and a footprint of 210 m^2. In the tradition of Tokyo's "sunshine law" that requires new buildings not to block more than a certain percentage of neighbors' light, Ando crafted the form until he found the ideal solution. Just under ten meters tall, the dark steel building is painted with zinc-based primer fluoropolymer paint. Just as the 4 x 4 House II will surprise certain people, so too will the hhstyle.com/casa building, but for different reasons. Ando shows here that he can be a virtuoso with materials other than concrete.

Das Tokioter Stadtgebiet zwischen Omotesando und Harajuku ist in architektonischer Hinsicht derzeit vielleicht das weltweit interessanteste mit Bauten von Herzog & de Meuron (Prada), Kengo Kuma (LVMH), Toyo Ito (Tod's) und Kazuyo Sejima (Dior). Ando arbeitet momentan (2005/06) noch an einem anderen, größeren Projekt in der Nähe. Hier hat er aus 16 mm dicken Stahlplatten einen ungewöhnlichen, wie ein Origami wirkenden Bau geschaffen. Mit 352 m^2 ist das Grundstück zwar nach Tokioter Standards relativ weitläufig, dennoch durften hier baugesetzlich nur maximal zweigeschossige Gebäude mit Stahl- oder Holzkonstruktionen errichtet werden. Noch dazu besteht die Gesamtfläche aus zwei Parzellen, deren eine für zehn Jahre und deren andere nur für fünf Jahre unter Pachtvertrag steht. Der Architekt musste also das Hauptbauvolumen auf dem für

zehn Jahre gepachteten Grundstücksteil planen. Das Designergeschäft hat eine Gesamtfläche von 469 m^2 über ein Untergeschoss und zwei Hochgeschosse auf einer Grundfläche von 210 m^2. In der Tradition von Tokios "Sonnenscheingesetz" (Neubauten dürfen Nachbargebäude nicht mehr als nach einem bestimmten Prozentsatz beschatten) entwickelte Ando verschiedene Alternativen, bis er die ideale Gebäudeform fand. Die dunklen Stahlfassaden des knapp 10 m hohen Baus sind mit zinkhaltiger Fluoropolymergrundierung gestrichen. Nicht nur das Haus 4 x 4 Nr. II wird einige Betrachter überraschen, sondern auch dieses Gebäude – aber aus jeweils unterschiedlichen Gründen. Ando zeigt hier nämlich, dass er nicht nur mit Beton, sondern auch mit anderen Baustoffen virtuos umgehen kann.

L'une des zones les plus intéressantes au monde, pour ce qui touche à l'architecture contemporaine, s'étend peut-être bien à Tokyo entre Omotesando et Harajuku. Herzog & de Meuron (Prada), Kengo Kuma (LVMH), Toyo Ito (Tod's) et Kazuyo Sejima (Dior) y sont tous représentés. En dehors d'un chantier en cours plus important à proximité, Ando vient d'apporter à ce quartier une nouvelle contribution sous forme d'un origami en plaques d'acier de 16 mm d'épaisseur. Bien que le terrain soit relativement vaste selon les critères tokyoïtes (352 m^2), la hauteur des constructions à ossature d'acier ou de bois est limitée à deux niveaux. De plus, le bail concerne une partie du terrain pour dix ans, l'autre pour cinq ans. Le client a donc demandé à l'architecte de réaliser l'essentiel du projet sur la partie louée pour dix ans. Sur deux niveaux et un sous-sol en continuité, ce magasin de design dispose d'une surface totale de 469 m^2 pour une emprise au sol de 210 m^2. Selon la règle de la « loi du soleil » tokyoïte qui interdit de bloquer plus qu'un certain pourcentage de l'éclairage naturel des constructions voisines, Ando a étudié avec soin la forme pour arriver à la solution idéale. De moins de 10 m de haut, son bâtiment en acier sombre est enduit d'une peinture aux fluoropolymères sur base zinguée. Comme pour la 4 x 4 House II, il peut surprendre certains, mais pour des raisons différentes. Ando montre ici sa virtuosité dans des matériaux autres que le béton.

The interior space of the store, now filled with design furniture and objects, has a slightly more cavernous and complex feeling than most Ando buildings. Metal and concrete meet in unexpected ways, particularly since Ando is not known to favor metal as a main construction material.

Das Ladeninnere – heute mit Designmöbeln und -objekten angefüllt – vermittelt einen höhlenartigeren und komplexeren Eindruck als die meisten anderen Bauten von Ando. Metall und Beton verbinden sich auf überraschende, für Ando untypische Weise, da der Architekt Metall generell nicht als Hauptbaumaterial einsetzt.

L'intérieur du magasin, aujourd'hui rempli de mobilier et d'objets de designers, donne une impression plus caverneuse et complexe que la plupart des réalisations de Ando. Le métal et le béton se confrontent de façon inattendue, d'autant plus que l'architecte utilise assez rarement le métal en matériau principal.

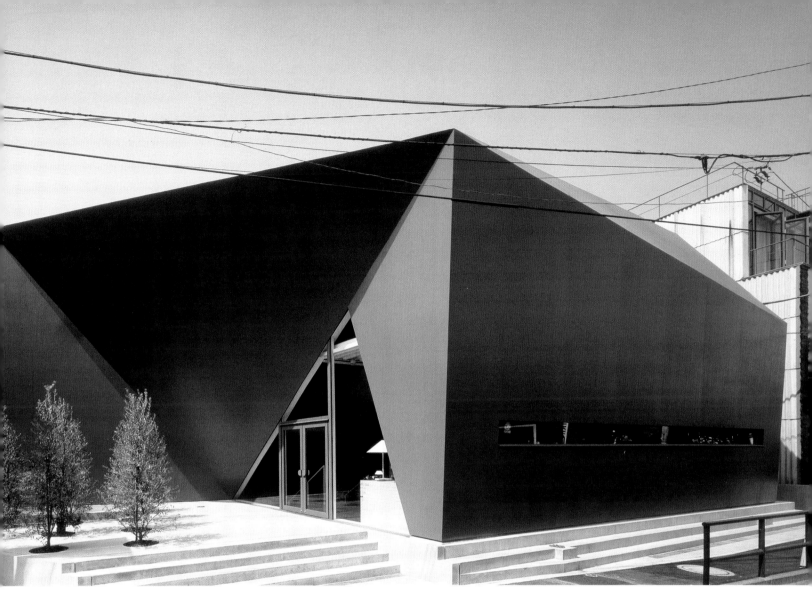

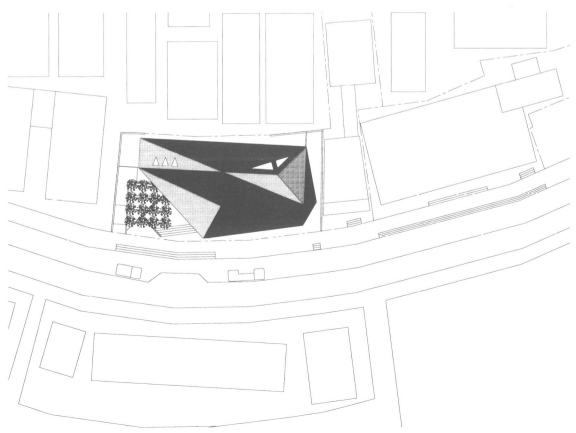

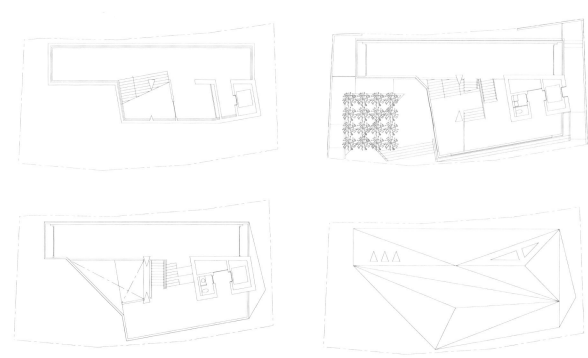

The folding interior spaces correspond to the relatively complex exterior and provide contrasts between the light near the entrance space (below) and the darker areas further into the shop. Austere grays and whites are used for interior finishes, allowing the objects displayed to stand out more easily in this strongly architectural environment.

Die mehrfach abgewinkelte Flucht der Innenräume entspricht der relativ komplexen äußeren Form und erzeugt Kontraste zwischen den hellen Bereichen nahe beim Eingang (unten) und den dunkleren in der Tiefe des Ladens. Die Einrichtung ist in Grau und Weiß gehalten, so dass die ausgestellten Gegenstände sich vor diesem strengen architektonischen Hintergrund gut abheben.

Les espaces intérieurs « repliés » répondent à la forme extérieure relativement complexe et génèrent un contraste entre la zone lumineuse de l'entrée (ci-dessous) et le reste du magasin, plus sombre. Des gris et des blancs austères ont été utilisés pour les finitions, permettant aux objets présentés de se détacher plus aisément de cet environnement très architecturé.

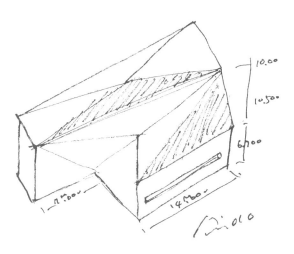

JUN AOKI

JUN AOKI & ASSOCIATES
#701 Harajuku New Royal Building
3-38-11, Jingumae
Shibuya-ku
Tokyo 150-0001

Tel: + 81 3 54 14 34 71
Fax: + 81 3 34 78 05 08
e-mail: info@aokijun.com
Web: aokijun.com

Born in 1956 in Yokohama, **JUN AOKI** graduated from the University of Tokyo in 1980, completed the Master Course in Architecture two years later, and became a registered architect in 1983. He worked in the office of Arata Isozaki (1983–90) and created his own firm, Jun Aoki & Associates, in 1991. He has lectured at Tokyo University (1995–98); the Tokyo Institute of Technology (1998–2000); and the Tokyo National University of Fine Arts and Music (1999–2001). His work includes: H House, Katsuura, Chiba (1994); O House, Setagaya, Tokyo (1996); Yusuikan swimming pool, Toyosaka, Niigata (1997); the Fukushima Lagoon Museum, Toyosaka, Niigata (1997); Louis Vuitton Nagoya, Nagoya, Aichi (1999); Louis Vuitton Ginza exterior design, Ginza, Tokyo (2000); Louis Vuitton New York exterior design, New York (2001–); and the Bird Feather Building shopping complex, Ginza, Tokyo (2003–). He won the Tokyo House Prize in 1994 for the H House, and the 1999 Architectural Institute of Japan Annual Award for the Fukushima Lagoon Museum. His Aomori Museum of Art, Aomori, opens in 2006. Jun Aoki has also worked actively as an artist, winning the Minister of Education's Art Encouragement Prize in 2005.

LOUIS VUITTON ROPPONGI HILLS
TOKYO
2002 · 06

FLOOR AREA: 1147 m², retail space 865 m²
CLIENT: Louis Vuitton Malletier
COST: not disclosed

If you give him a little more time, Jun Aoki may become the "official" designer of Louis Vuitton, having completed the façades of their very visible flagship stores in Omotesando in Tokyo and on 57th Street and Fifth Avenue in New York. One of his latest ventures for the French luxury-goods group is their Roppongi Hills shop. Located in the massive Roppongi Hills Keyakizaka Complex designed by KPF and completed in 2003, the new shop has a total floor area of 1 147 m². The design of this project is the result of a collaboration between three designers: Jun Aoki & Associates, Eric Carlson of Louis Vuitton, and Aurelio Clementi. The interest of Jun Aoki focuses on the use of a repetitive geometric form to obtain the relatively complex results seen here. As he says, "Louis Vuitton Roppongi Hills is a store designed, on both the inside and the outside, as a collection of simple circular units 10 centimeters in diameter. On the exterior wall, over 28 000 transparent glass tubes, 10 centimeters in diameter and 30 centimeters in length and sealed between two plates of glass, are suspended by two reflective stainless-steel panels in which holes of the same diameter have been cut. These elements, which resemble a compound eye, cause diffuse reflections. They pick up nearby lights and colors and change subtly in appearance. The interior is divided into a 'plaza' and a 'salon'; a skin made from a combination of stainless-steel rings, 10 centimeters in diameter, defines the boundary between them. The spatial form of the store has been deliberately made complex. The repetitive use of a simple element generates both a sense of unity and diversity."

Wenn man noch ein bisschen Zeit abwartet, wird Jun Aoki eines Tages vielleicht Chefarchitekt der Firma Louis Vuitton, da er bereits die Fassaden ihrer Flagg-schiff-Läden im Tokioter Omotesando-Viertel und an der New Yorker 57th Street/ Ecke Fifth Avenue gestaltet hat. Eines seiner letzten Projekte für die französische Luxusmarke ist ihr neues Geschäft im Roppongi-Viertel von Tokio. Es befindet sich im 2003 fertig gestellten massiven Roppongi Hills Keyakizaka-Komplex der Architekten KPF und hat eine Gesamtfläche von 1147 m². Die Innenausstattung ist das Gemeinschaftswerk von drei Gestaltern: Jun Aoki & Associates, Eric Carlson von Louis Vuitton und Aurelio Clementi. Aoki war vor allem an der Entwicklung einer seriellen geometrischen Form interessiert, um ein relativ komplexes Resultat zu erzielen, wie man am Ergebniss sieht. Zu seinem Entwurf schrieb er: „Louis Vuitton Roppongi Hills ist eine Boutique, die innen wie außen mit einer Ansammlung von einfachen runden Elementen mit jeweils 10 cm Durchmesser gestaltet ist. Außen bestehen die Fassadenmodule aus über 28 000 Klarglasröhrchen (Durchmesser 10 cm, 30 cm lang) zwischen zwei Glasplatten. Diese sind an zwei reflektierenden Platten befestigt, in die Löcher mit identischem Durchmesser eingeschnitten sind. Die Elemente ähneln Facettenaugen und erzeugen diffuse Lichtreflexe. Sie spiegeln Licht und Farben aus der Umgebung und verändern dadurch auf subtile Weise ihr Aussehen. Innen ist der Laden mit Hilfe eines Raumteilers aus Stahlringen (Durchmesser 10 cm) in ‚Plaza' und ‚Salon' unterteilt. Die Vielgestaltigkeit der Innenausstattung und räumlichen Gliederung war Absicht. Die Wiederholung eines einfachen Elements sorgt für Einheitlichkeit und Vielfalt zugleich."

Avec un peu plus de temps, Jun Aoki qui vient d'achever les façades des magasins Louis Vuitton d'Omotesando à Tokyo, de la 57th Street et de la Fifth Avenue à New York, pourrait bien devenir le designer «officiel» de la marque. L'une de ses dernières réalisations pour le groupe français est son magasin de Roppongi Hills. Situées dans l'énorme complexe Keyakizaka des collines de Roppongi, conçu par KPF et achevé en 2003, les nouvelles installations mesurent 1147 m². Leur conception est le fruit d'une collaboration entre trois intervenants, Jun Aoki & Associates, Eric Carlson de Louis Vuitton et Aurelio Clementi. Jun Aoki aime à se concentrer sur l'utilisations de motifs géométriques répétitifs pour obtenir un résultat assez complexe, comme ici. Il explique : « Le magasin Louis Vuitton est conçu aussi bien à l'intérieur qu'à l'extérieur comme un assemblage de simples éléments circulaires de 10 cm de diamètre. Sur le mur extérieur, plus de 28 000 tubes de verre transparent de 10 cm de diamètre et de 30 de long, scellés entre deux plaques de verre, sont suspendus par deux panneaux d'acier inoxydable réfléchissant dans lesquels des trous d'un même diamètre ont été percés. Ces éléments, qui ressemblent à un œil composé, provoquent des réflexions diffuses. Ils prennent la lumière et les couleurs de l'environnement et changent subtilement d'aspect. L'intérieur se répartit entre une ‹ plazza › et un ‹ salon › dont la frontière est matérialisée par une peau composée d'anneaux en acier inoxydable de 10 cm de diamètre. La forme spatiale du magasin a été délibérément rendue complexe. L'utilisation répétitive d'un élément simple génère un sentiment à la fois d'unité et de diversité. »

Jun Aoki's main contribution to the spectacular Louis Vuitton shop in Roppongi Hills is the exterior façade. With its shimmering glass "curtain" of tubes, the architecture makes way for a large-scale inscription of the French firm's name.

Jun Aokis Hauptbeitrag zur spektakulären Louis-Vuitton-Boutique in Roppongi Hills ist die Fassade mit ihrem glänzenden „Vorhang" aus Glasröhren, der mit dem Namenszug der französischen Luxusmarke im Großformat versehen ist.

La principale contribution de Jun Aoki au spectaculaire magasin Louis Vuitton de Roppongi Hills est la façade extérieure. Le « rideau » de tubes de verre miroitant s'efface au bénéfice du nom de la marque traité à grande échelle.

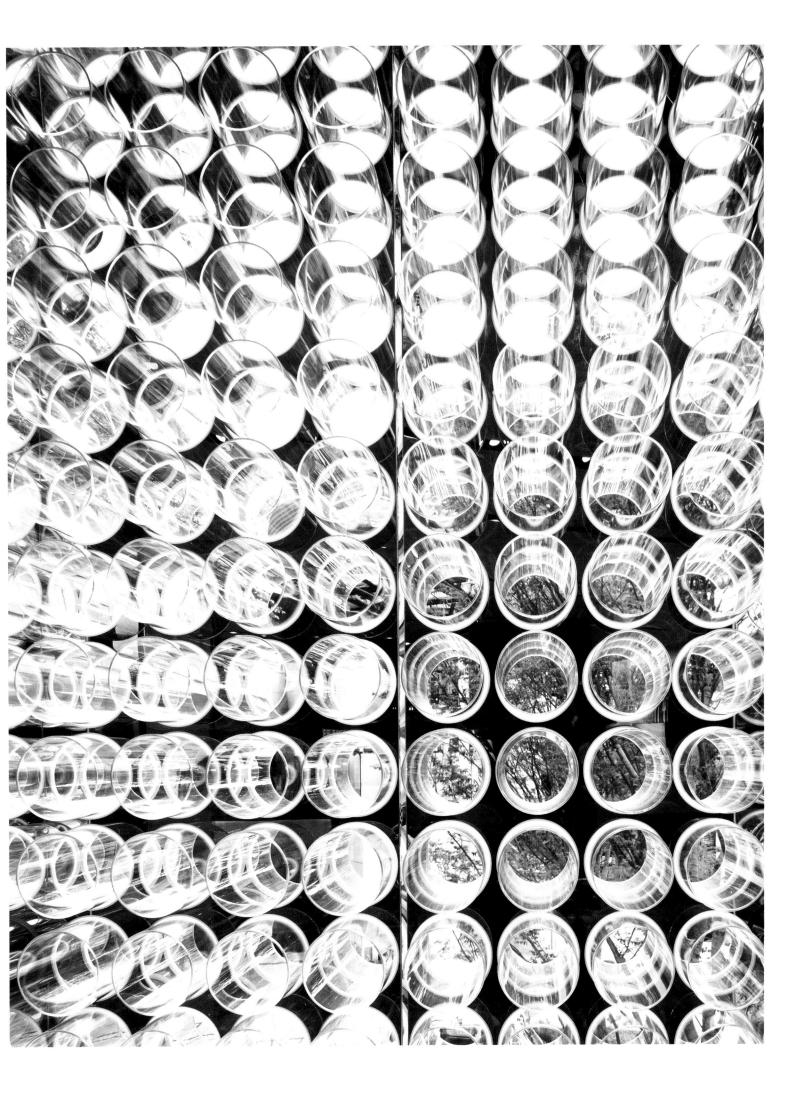

The "skin" between the two main interior areas of the shop, made of stainless-steel rings is Jun Aoki's contribution to a design that was also worked on by Eric Carlson of Louis Vuitton and Aurelio Clementi.

Die „Häute" zwischen den beiden Hauptverkaufsräumen des Ladens bestehen aus Edelstahlringen – ein weiterer Beitrag von Jun Aoki zu einem Ladendesign, an dem auch Eric Carlson von Louis Vuitton und Aurelio Clementi mitwirkten.

La « peau » en anneaux d'acier inoxydable tendue entre les deux principales zones du magasin est une contribution de Jun Aoki à un projet auquel ont également participé Eric Carlson de chez Louis Vuitton et Aurelio Clementi.

SHIGERU BAN

SHIGERU BAN ARCHITECTS
5-2-4, Matsubara
Setagaya-ku
Tokyo 156-0043

Tel: + 81 3 33 24 67 60
Fax: + 81 3 33 24 67 89
e-mail:
tokyo@shigerubanarchitects.com
Web: www.shigerubanarchitects.com

Born in 1957 in Tokyo, **SHIGERU BAN** studied at the Southern California Institute of Architecture (SCI-Arc) from 1977 to 1980. He attended the Cooper Union School of Architecture, where he studied under John Hejduk (1980–82). He worked in the office of Arata Isozaki (1982–83) before founding his own firm in Tokyo in 1985. His work includes numerous exhibition designs (Alvar Aalto show at the Axis Gallery, Tokyo, 1986). His buildings include: the Odawara Pavilion, Kanagawa (1990); the Paper Gallery, Tokyo (1994); the Paper House, Lake Yamanaka (1995); and the Paper Church, Takatori, Hyogo (1995). He has also designed ephemeral structures, such as his Paper Refugee Shelter made with plastic sheets and paper tubes for the United Nations High Commission for Refugees (UNHCR). He designed the Japanese Pavilion at Expo 2000, Hanover. Current work includes: a small museum of Canal History in Pouilly-en-Auxois, France; the Schwartz Residence, Sharon, Connecticut; the Forest Park Pavilion—Bamboo Gridshell-02, St Louis, Missouri; Mul(ti)houses, Mulhouse, France; the Sagaponac House/ Furniture House-05, Long Island, New York; and the Hanegi Forest Annex, Setagaya, Tokyo. He installed his Temporary Paper Studio featured here, on top of the Centre Georges Pompidou in Paris to work on the new Centre Pompidou in Metz, France.

SHUTTER HOUSE FOR A PHOTOGRAPHER
TOKYO
2002 - 03

FLOOR AREA: 465 m²
CLIENT: Yoshihiko Ueda
COST: not disclosed

Designed for a successful photographer, this house is unusual in that it has a long, rectangular plot of land, and a considerable floor area by Japanese standards (465 m²). The actual building covers only 142 m², however. Made of concrete, steel-reinforced concrete, and steel, it is part of a series of buildings designed by Shigeru Ban with rolling shutters that can be opened completely when weather allows. Ultimately, these shutters can serve to dissolve the boundaries between interior and exterior. The photographer told the architect, "If only Mies had been alive, I would have commissioned him ..." Ban's response was to create strict grid modules, four meters and two meters on a side that make up all of the rooms and the interior courtyards. A canopy of thin louvers and full-height glazing facing the inner courtyards provides ample natural light. A high checkerboard screen with vegetation growing from it surrounds the house on all sides to give sufficient privacy. A large underground studio protected from the light was designed for the photographer. With typical humor, Ban says, "I was relieved, after the completion, to hear the client say, in a casual manner 'it was better than asking Mies to do it.'"

Dieses Haus für einen erfolgreichen Fotografen ist insofern ungewöhnlich, als es auf einem langen, rechteckigen Grundstück steht und nach japanischen Maßstäben mit 465 m² Gesamtfläche gewaltige Ausmaße hat. Die Grundfläche beträgt allerdings nur 142 m². Das Gebäude besteht aus Beton, Stahlbeton und Stahl und gehört zu einer Reihe von Häusern, die Shigeru Ban mit Rollläden ausgestattet hat, die bei schönem Wetter ganz hochgezogen werden können und letztlich dazu beitragen, die Grenzen zwischen Innen- und Außenraum aufzuheben. Der Bauherr erklärte dem Architekten: „Wenn Mies noch am Leben wäre, hätte ich ihn beauftragt." Ban tat, was er konnte, und schuf ein Haus mit streng rechtwinkligem Grundrissraster auf der Basis von 4 x 2 m großen Rastermodulen für sämtliche Räume und Innenhöfe. Ein Baldachin aus dünnen Latten und raumhohe Glaswände um die Höfe sorgen für eine helle, natürliche Beleuchtung der Innenräume. Eine hohe Wand mit abwechselnd offenen und begrünten „Schachbrettfeldern" umgibt das Haus auf allen Seiten und sorgt für ausreichend Sichtschutz. Im Untergeschoss baute Ban nach den Wünschen des Fotografen ein großes Atelier mit Dunkelkammer ein. Mit dem ihm eigenen Humor sagte Ban: „Ich war ganz erleichtert, als der Bauherr nach der Fertigstellung so nebenbei äußerte, es sei noch besser geworden, als wenn er Mies beauftragt hätte."

Conçue pour un photographe connu, cette maison est inhabituelle, du moins selon les critères japonais puisqu'elle mesure 465 m² et s'élève sur une vaste parcelle rectangulaire allongée. Son emprise au sol n'est cependant que de 142 m². En béton, béton armé et acier, elle fait partie d'une série de réalisations de Shigeru Ban, dotées de volets roulants qui peuvent s'ouvrir totalement lorsque le temps le permet. Au final, ce principe abolit les frontières classiques entre le dedans et le dehors. Le photographe avait simplement dit à l'architecte : « Si Mies van der Rohe était encore vivant, je lui aurais demandé de réaliser cette maison ... » La réponse de Ban fut une trame de modules de 4 x 2 m, appliquée à l'ensemble des pièces et des cours intérieures. Un écran composé de fines jalousies et de panneaux de verre toute hauteur donnant sur la cour intérieure apporte un généreux éclairage naturel dans la maison. Un écran en damier végétalisé entoure celle-ci sur toutes ses faces pour assurer l'intimité nécessaire. Le vaste studio souterrain protégé de la lumière était souhaité par le photographe. Avec son humour typique, Ban fait remarquer : « Une fois le chantier fini, j'ai été heureux d'entendre le client lancer : ‹ C'est encore mieux que si je l'avais demandé à Mies ›. »

The simple, elegant entrance façade of the house allows for just one tree within its screened boundary. The side walls are covered with vines growing from planters inserted into the façades.

Die schlichte, elegante Eingangsfassade des Hauses umgibt einen einzelnen Baum. Die Seitenmauern sind begrünt: Kletterpflanzen wachsen aus in die Außenmauern eingelassenen Pflanzgefäßen empor.

L'élégante et simple façade d'entrée de la maison n'autorisait la présence que d'un seul arbre entre les écrans qui marquent ses limites. Les murs latéraux sont recouverts de vigne grimpante s'élevant de jardinières insérées dans les façades.

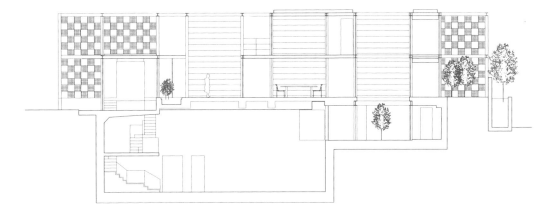

The interior space is furnished in a modern style and the interior courtyards with sliding glass walls that can be opened fully in summer bring a feeling of natural space into a house located in the heart of Tokyo.

Das Innere ist modern eingerichtet; Innenhöfe mit Glasschiebetüren, die sich im Sommer vollständig öffnen lassen, bringen ein Gefühl von Naturnähe in dieses Haus im Zentrum von Tokio.

L'intérieur est meublé en style moderne. Les cours intérieures aux parois de verre coulissantes entièrement ouvrables en été apportent le sentiment de la nature dans une maison qui se trouve cependant au cœur de Tokyo.

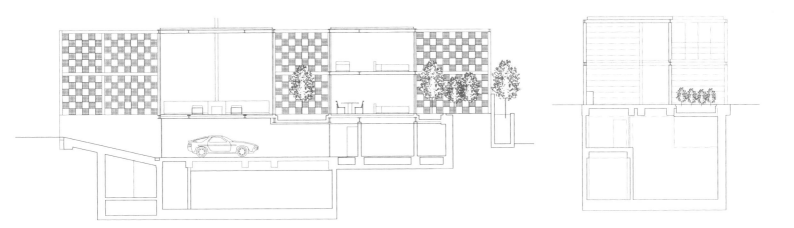

The photographer's ample underground studio (left) maintains the white simplicity found elsewhere but excludes natural light. Opposite is the living room on the ground floor, a small entrance room (below left) and the stairway leading down to the studio (below right).

Das geräumige Kellerstudio des Fotografen (rechte Seite) setzt die weiße Schlichtheit der übrigen Räume fort, nur ohne Tageslicht. Die Abbildungen auf dieser Seite zeigen das Wohnzimmer im Erdgeschoss, eine kleine Diele (unten links) und die Treppe zum Kellerstudio (unten rechts).

Le vaste studio souterrain du photographe (à gauche) reproduit la simplicité de la blancheur immaculée du reste de la maison, mais sans lumière naturelle. Page de droite, le séjour au rez-de-chaussée, une petite pièce d'entrée (en bas, à gauche) et l'escalier qui descend vers le studio (en bas, à droite).

GLASS SHUTTER HOUSE TOKYO 2001-02

FLOOR AREA: 152 m²
CLIENT: Yashiharu Doi
COST: not disclosed

Located in the Meguro area of Tokyo, this combined residence and restaurant is located on a small, 139 m² site. It was built for a chef well known for his television appearances and his cooking school, also located in the new structure. The building area is just 73 m² and total floor area is 152 m². The three-story 4 x 16 meter steel-frame house is remarkable because two of its façades open entirely from street level to roof. Rolling glass shutters disappear into the roof, allowing an outside patio with a bamboo wall to become an integral part of the restaurant in warm weather. Local regulations normally permit only two stories on this site but, as Shigeru Ban says, "The three-story volume which has only two floors is legally considered to be two-storied. The stairs connecting to the second level legally mean a floor dividing the first and the second floor. The whole volume is equivalent to three ordinary stories. The completed building has a restaurant on the ground floor, a kitchen studio on the second and housing on the third floor. Each area vertically conveys a sense of unity and the border-line, workplace or housing, is intentionally unclear." Ban concludes, "I have tried to connect inner space to the outside by using consecutive outward-opening doors in a series of housing projects. The shutters can be fully opened or be set at the height of each floor, which enables inner space to connect to outside in various ways and to be barrier free. Also, the fence made of bamboo defines the border to the neighboring site and secures its privacy." Because of its refined support design, the Glass Shutter House is extremely light and airy, giving new meaning to the typical Japanese idea of "in-between space."

Das im Tokioter Wohnviertel Meguro auf einem nur 139 m² großen Grundstück gelegene Gebäude ist eine Kombination aus Wohnhaus und Restaurant. Es wurde für einen Koch entworfen, der für seine Kochsendung im Fernsehen und seine – ebenfalls im Haus untergebrachte – Kochschule bekannt ist. Die Grundfläche des Hauses beträgt nur 73 m²; die gesamt Fläche 152 m². Als besonderes Merkmal der dreigeschossigen, 4 x 16 m messenden Stahlrahmenkonstruktion lassen sich zwei seiner Fassaden vom Erdgeschoss bis zum Dach vollkommen öffnen, indem man die Glasjalousien ins Dach hochziehen kann, wodurch der offene Hof zu einem Teil des Restaurants wird. Zwar erlauben die lokalen Bauvorschriften an diesem Standort nur zwei Stockwerke, doch gilt das eigentlich dreigeschossige Haus durch die Treppe, die den ersten mit dem zweiten Stock verbindet, rechtlich als zweistöckig. Im Erdgeschoss befindet sich das Restaurant, während im ersten Stock eine Studioküche und auf den oberen Ebenen die Wohnräume liegen. Die vertikale Anordnung dieser Bereiche vermittelt einen zusammenhängenden Eindruck, wobei zwischen Arbeiten und Wohnen bewusst nicht klar getrennt wurde. Auch in anderer Hinsicht wurden Grenzen offen gelassen, wie Shigeru Ban erläutert: „Ich habe bereits zuvor bei einer Reihe von Wohnhäusern versucht, Innen und Außen durch Türen zu verbinden. Hier sind es die Jalousien, die ganz oder einzeln geöffnet werden können, wodurch sich die Innenräume auf unterschiedliche Weise und nahtlos mit der äußeren Umgebung verbinden lassen. Ansonsten wird durch den Bambuszaun die Grenze zum Nachbargrundstück definiert und damit die Privatsphäre gewahrt." Aufgrund seines ausgeklügelten Tragwerks ist das Glas Shutter House äußerst leicht und luftig gebaut, was dem typisch japanischen Gedanken vom „Zwischen-Raum" eine neue Bedeutung verleiht.

Située à Tokyo, dans le quartier de Meguro, cette maison qui associe un restaurant et un logement, occupe un petit terrain de 139 m². Elle a été construite à l'intention d'un cuisinier connu pour ses émissions de télévision et son école de cuisine, installée à la même adresse. L'emprise au sol n'est que de 73 m² et la surface utile de 152 m². Cette construction de trois niveaux, à ossature d'acier et mesurant 4 x 16 m, étonne par ses deux façades qui s'ouvrent entièrement, du niveau de la rue jusqu'au toit. D'énormes volets roulants de verre disparaissent dans la couverture, ce qui permet à un patio extérieur à clôture de bambou de venir agrandir le restaurant à la belle saison. La réglementation locale n'autorisait que deux niveaux, mais comme l'explique Shigeru Ban : « Le volume sur trois niveaux mais avec deux planchers intérieurs est légalement considéré comme une maison à un seul étage. Il équivaut à deux étages ordinaires. La structure comprend le restaurant au rez-de-chaussée, l'école au premier et le logement au deuxième étage. Verticalement chaque zone exprime une impression d'unité et la limite entre logement et travail reste volontairement floue. » Il conclut : « J'avais déjà essayé de relier l'espace intérieur et extérieur par différents types de portes ouvrant sur l'extérieur dans de précédents projets. Les volets roulants peuvent s'ouvrir en grand ou seulement à la hauteur de chaque niveau, ce qui offre au volume intérieur des connexion variées avec l'extérieur, sans barrière. La clôture de bambou définit la frontière avec le terrain voisin et assure l'intimité. » Grâce à son dessin raffiné, cette maison extrêmement légère et aérée donne un sens nouveau au concept japonais traditionnel d'espace « entre-deux ».

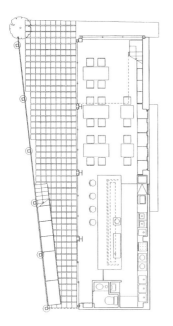 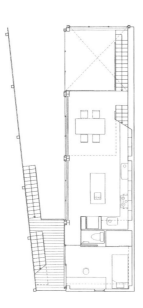 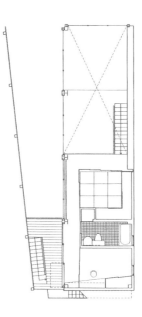

The sides of the restaurant and residence open fully in summer, allowing the outdoor terrace to communicate freely with the interior. The rolling shutters are stored in the open position in the overhang visible in the image below.

Im Sommer lassen sich Restaurant und Wohnhaus seitlich vollständig öffnen, so dass der Innenraum nahtlos in die Gartenterrasse übergeht. Die Rollläden verschwinden dann in den vorstehenden Kästen, die im Bild unten zu sehen sind.

Les côtés du restaurant et de la résidence s'ouvrent intégralement en été, ce qui permet à la terrasse extérieure de communiquer librement avec l'intérieur. Les volets roulants se replient en position fermée dans le porte-à-faux visible ci-dessous.

SHUHEI ENDO

SHUHEI ENDO ARCHITECTURE INSTITUTE
Domus AOI 5F
5-15-11, Nishitenma
Kita-ku
Osaka 530-0047

Tel: +81 6 63 12-74 55
Fax: +81 6 63 12-74 56
e-mail: endo@paramodern.com
Web: www.paramodern.com

Born in Shiga Prefecture in 1960, **SHUHEI ENDO** obtained his master's degree from the Kyoto City University of Art in 1986. He worked after that with the architect Osamu Ishii and established his own firm, the Shuhei Endo Architecture Institute, in 1988. His work has been widely published and he has received numerous prizes, including the Andrea Palladio International Prize in Italy (1993). He showed a sculptural work called "Springtecture Orléans" (1999–2000) during the city's Archilab exhibition. His recent work includes: Slowtecture S, Maihara, Shiga (2002); Growtecture S, Osaka (2002); Springtecture B, Biwa-cho, Shiga (2002); Bubbletecture M, Maihara, Shiga (2003); Rooftecture C, Taishi, Hyogo (2003); Rooftecture H, Kamigori, Hyogo (2004); and Bubbletecture O, Maruoka, Fukui (2004). A monograph on his work entitled *Shuhei Endo, Paramodern Architecture* was published in 2003.

SPRINGTECTURE O-RUSH TENPAKU
NAGOYA
2005

FLOOR AREA: 283 m^2
CLIENT: TCLA
COST: $850 000

This two-story used-car dealer and garage covers 214 m^2 of an 880 m^2 site. Its total floor area is 283 m^2. Made with steel sheet, this building, unlike others in Endo's "Springtecture" series, is made up of two perpendicular bands. The reason for this was to create greater structural strength and to allow for differentiated space. Endo explains that "Composed of continuous bands, the studies in 'Springtecture' seek to acquire an 'independence' of space where its division is not defined by function. Instead, 'Springtecture' forms space as the continuous band moves to define floor, ceiling, and roof simultaneously. This continuity and reversal of the double-faced surface allows for a connection between outside and inside without any abrupt differentiation. As a result, 'Springtecture' achieves a variable structure of openness and closure, in contrast with the surrounding homogeneous townscape." Where other architects have sought to achieve a certain fluidity of form through the extensive use of computers and new materials, Endo takes a relatively common material and turns it into an unusual building without recourse to complex parametric modeling.

Das zweigeschossige Gebäude mit Verkaufsraum für Gebrauchtwagen und Werkstatt nimmt 214 m^2 eines 880 m^2 großen Grundstücks ein mit einer gesamten Geschossfläche von 283 m^2. Anders als Endos übrige Bauten seiner „Springtecture"-Serie besteht dieses im Wesentlichen aus zwei im rechten Winkel zueinander gesetzten Stahlplattenbändern. Auf diese Weise wollte der Architekt größere konstruktive Festigkeit erzielen und differenzierte Räume schaffen. „Mit den ‚Springtecture'-Experimenten aus fortlaufenden Bändern versuche ich die ‚Unabhängigkeit' des Raums zu erzielen, bei der die Raumgliederung nicht durch die Funktion bestimmt wird", erklärt Endo. „Stattdessen bildet ‚Springtecture' Raum, während das Band sich vorwärts bewegt, um zeitgleich Boden, Decke und Dach zu umschreiben. Diese Kontinuität und die Umkehr der beidseitig identischen Oberfläche ermöglicht die Schaffung einer Verbindung von Innen und Außen ohne jede abrupte Unterscheidung. Daher erzielt ‚Springtecture' eine variable Struktur – Offenheit und Geschlossenheit – im Gegensatz zur benachbarten homogenen Stadtlandschaft." Während andere Architekten mit Hilfe des computergestützten Designs und mit neuen Materialien eine fließende Form zu schaffen versuchen, nimmt Endo einen relativ gewöhnlichen Baustoff und macht daraus ohne kompliziertes parametrisches Modellieren ein ungewöhnliches Gebäude.

Ce magasin et garage pour voitures d'occasion occupe 214 m^2 d'un terrain de 880 m^2, mais sa surface totale utile est de 283 m^2. Fait de tôles d'acier ondulé, ce bâtiment sur deux niveaux, à la différence d'autres de la série « Springtecture » de Endo est constitué de deux bandes perpendiculaires. La raison en est à rechercher du côté de la nécessité d'obtenir la plus grande résistance structurelle possible et de permettre une plus grande différenciation des espaces. Endo explique que « composée de bandeaux continus, l'étude de ‹ Springtecture › cherche à générer une ‹ indépendance › de l'espace dont la division n'est pas définie par sa fonction. En fait, ‹ Springtecture › constitue son propre espace au fur et à mesure que le bandeau continu se développe pour définir simultanément le sol, le plafond et la toiture. Cette continuité et l'inversion de surfaces à double-face permettent une connexion entre l'intérieur et l'extérieur sans différenciation abrupte. Il en résulte une structure à ouverture et fermeture variables par rapport à une environnement urbain homogène ». Quand d'autres architectes cherchent à obtenir une certaine fluidité de formes en recourant aux ordinateurs et aux nouveaux matériaux, Endo s'empare d'une matériau relativement banal et le transforme en une construction étonnante sans le moindre recours à la complexité paramétrique des modélisations.

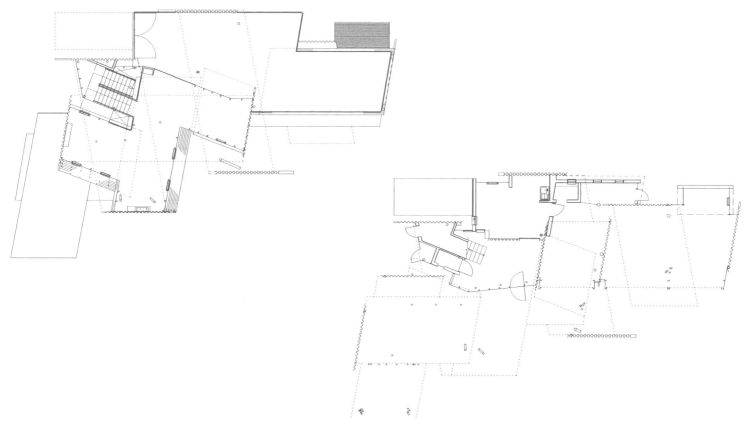

The architect has worked extensively with the idea of forming buildings from a continuous band of corrugated steel but, in this instance, he reaches a high degree of complexity and aesthetic surprise.

Der Architekt hat sich mehrfach eingehend mit der Idee beschäftigt, Gebäude aus einem fortlaufenden Band aus Wellblech zu gestalten. In diesem Fall hat er dabei ein hohes Maß an Komplexität und ästhetischen Überraschungen erzielt.

L'architecte a beaucoup travaillé sur des projets de constructions à partir de bandes continues d'acier ondulé, mais il a atteint ici à un haut degré particulièrement élevé de complexité et de surprise esthétique.

The fact that Shuhei Endo masters the unusual structural innovations of this building is perhaps most visible in the interiors, which are certainly metallic in appearance, but ample and easily usable.

Die meisterhafte Umsetzung der ungewöhnlichen konstruktiven Innovationen in diesem Gebäude von Shuhei Endo lässt sich vielleicht am deutlichsten an seinen geräumigen Innenräumen ablesen, die zwar viel Metall zeigen, aber dennoch wohnlich sind.

La maîtrise par Shuhei Endo des implications de ses innovations structurelles est particulièrement visible dans les espaces intérieurs qui restent généreux et facilement utilisables bien que d'aspect très métallique.

MASAKI ENDOH AND MASAHIRO IKEDA

MASAKI ENDOH
EDH Endoh Design House
2-13-8, Honnmachi
Shibuya-ku / Tokyo 151-0071
Tel/Fax: + 81 3 33 77 62 93
e-mail: endoh@edh-web.com
Web: www.edh-web.com

MASAHIRO IKEDA CO., LTD
MIAS Masahiro Ikeda Architecture Studio
201 Silhouette-Ohyamacho
1-20, Ohyama-cho
Shibuya-ku / Tokyo 151-0065
Tel: + 81 3 57 38 55 64
Fax: + 81 3 57 38 55 65
e-mail: info@miascoltd.net
Web: www.miascoltd.net

MASAKI ENDOH was born in Tokyo, in 1963. He graduated from the Science University of Tokyo in 1987 and completed the Master Course of Architecture in 1989, at the same University. He worked the KAI-Workshop (1989–94) and established his firm EDH Endoh Design House in 1994. He is currently a lecturer at the Science University of Tokyo. He was awarded the Tokyo House Prize for "Natural Shelter" in 2000, the Yoshioka Award for "Natural Shelter" in 2000, the JIA "Rookie of the Year 2003" for "Natural Ellipse" in 2003. His works include: Natural Shelter, Tokyo (1999); Natural Illuminance, Tokyo (2001); Natural Slats, Tokyo (2002); Natural Ellipse, Tokyo (2002); Natural Wedge (featured here, Tokyo, 2003); and Natural Strata, Kawasaki (2003).

MASAHIRO IKEDA was born in Shizuoka, in 1964. He graduated from the Nagoya University in 1987 and completed the School of Engineering at Nagoya University in 1989. He worked with Kimura Structural Engineers (1989–91) and Sasaki Structural Consultants (1991–94) before establishing his firm MIAS (Masahiro Ikeda Architecture Studio) in 1994. Masahiro Ikeda has acted as the structural designer for these houses. As Masaki Endoh says however, Masahiro Ikeda has played such a significant role in these projects that he, too, should be considered one of the architects.

NATURAL WEDGE

TOKYO
2002-03

FLOOR AREA: 84 m²
CLIENT: Yuji Hosizawa
COST: not disclosed

As is typically the case of Tokyo houses, the site for this residence for a young couple is tiny (58 m²). Endoh and Ikeda, working together here as they have for a number of small houses, sought a "novel approach to provide the house with a comfortable life." They imagined a wrapping or a "skin-like borderline" between interior and exterior. The steel-frame building with a footprint of only 34.5 m² and a total floor area of 84 m² has a decidedly unusual shape. As Endoh explains, "Its overall shape—a 45-degree triangle—was devised for compliance with legal height restriction and for maximum natural lighting inside the house that faces north. The same shape was adapted to the basic modules such as the slab floor." Endoh and Ikeda used a Goretex membrane between the external glass (with shatter-prevention film) and the polyester heat-insulation in order to provide UV protection to the residents. Heated maple flooring is used. Although the form of the Natural Wedge may seem extravagant to many people who do not know the real-estate market in central Tokyo, here it makes perfect sense. Indeed, Endoh and Ikeda continually show their capacity to craft intelligent responses to rather extreme size constraints.

Wie bei den meisten Einfamilienhäusern in Tokio stand auch für dieses Haus eines jungen Ehepaars nur ein winziges Grundstück zur Verfügung (58 m²). Endoh und Ikeda, die schon andere Häuser gemeinsam geplant hatten, suchten nach „neuen Wegen für ein komfortables Wohnen", und dachten an eine „hautähnliche Abgrenzung" zwischen Innen- und Außenraum. Das Haus mit Stahlrahmentragwerk auf einer Grundfläche von nur 34,5 m² und einer Gesamtgeschossfläche von 84 m² hat eine entschieden ungewöhnliche Form. „Seine Dreiecksform mit 45-Grad-Winkel wählten wir, um der gesetzlich vorgeschriebenen maximalen Gebäudehöhe zu entsprechen", so Endoh, „und um das nach Norden ausgerichtete Hausinnere mit möglichst viel Tageslicht zu versorgen." Die gleiche Form wurde für die Grundmodule wie etwa die Geschossdecken verwendet. Endoh und Ikeda entschieden sich für eine Goretex-Membran als Lage zwischen den äußeren Glasscheiben (mit Splitterschutzfilmbeschichtung) und der Wärmedämmlage aus Polyester, um die Bewohner vor UV-Einstrahlung zu schützen. Die Ahornböden sind mit Fußbodenheizung unterlegt. Vielen Betrachtern, die Tokios innerstädtischen Immobilienmarkt nicht kennen, mag die Form des „natürlichen Keils" extravant erscheinen, sie ist hier aber die einzig richtige Entscheidung. Endoh und Ikeda haben immer wieder bewiesen, dass sie in der Lage sind, auf kleinstem Raum intelligente Lösungen zu realisieren.

Comme très souvent le cas dans les maisons tokyoïtes, le terrain de cette résidence pour un jeune couple est minuscule : 58 m². Endoh et Tikeda, collaborant ici comme ils l'ont déjà fait pour plusieurs petites maisons, ont cherché « une nouvelle approche afin de permettre des conditions d'existence confortable dans cette maison ». Ils ont imaginé une enveloppe ou une « limite en forme de peau » entre l'intérieur et l'extérieur. L'ossature en acier (emprise au sol de 34,5 m² seulement et surface totale de 84 m²) présente une forme décidément inhabituelle. Comme l'explique Endoh : « La forme générale est un triangle à 45° adapté aux contraintes locales de hauteur, pour permettre une pénétration maximum de la lumière naturelle à l'intérieur de cette maison orientée au nord. La même forme a été adaptée aux modules de base, dont celui du sol dallé. » Les deux architectes ont posé une membrane en Goretex entre le verre extérieur (à film de sécurité intégré) et le doublage thermique en polyester qui protège des UV. Bien que la forme de cette maison puisse sembler extravagante à ceux qui ne connaissent pas la situation du marché immobilier au centre de Tokyo, elle est en réalité parfaitement censée. Endoh et Ikeda montrent ici, une fois encore, leur talent à fournir des réponses intelligentes à des contraintes dimensionnelles quasi extrêmes.

The translucent skin of the house glows at night, while it appears to be entirely opaque during the day. As plans and the images show, the wedge shape of the house dictates rapidly decreasing floor area on the upper levels, but natural light is omnipresent.

Bei Nacht leuchtet die transluzente Fassade des Hauses von innen, bei Tage erscheint sie vollkommen undurchsichtig. Die Pläne und Fotos machen deutlich, wie die Keilform des Hauses die Wohnfläche nach oben immer geringer werden lässt, aber auch in jedem Raum für natürliche Beleuchtung sorgt.

La peau translucide de la maison brille la nuit, mais semble entièrement opaque pendant le jour. Comme le montrent les plans et les photos, la forme en coin de la maison entraîne une réduction rapide de la surface du sol aux niveaux supérieurs, mais l'éclairage naturel reste omniprésent.

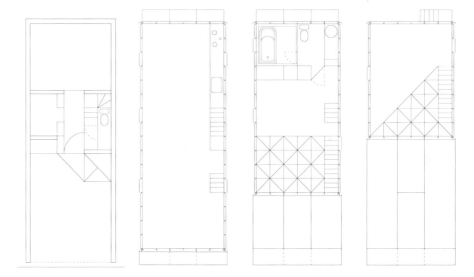

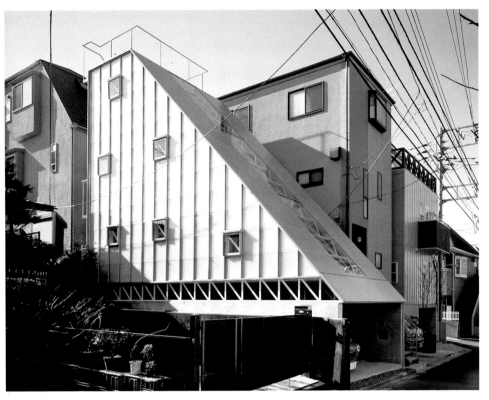

HIROSHI HARA

HIROSHI HARA + ATELIER
10-3, Hachiyama-cho
Shibuya-ku
Tokyo 150-0035

Tel: + 81 3 34 64 86 70
Fax: + 81 3 34 64 86 12
e-mail:
atelier-phi@mvg.biglobe.ne.jp

Born in Kawasaki in 1936, **HIROSHI HARA** received his Bachelor's degree from the University of Tokyo (1959), his Master's degree in 1961 and his Ph. D. degree from the same institution in 1964, before becoming an associate professor at the university's Faculty of Architecture. Though his first work dates from the early 1960s, he began his collaboration with Atelier in 1970. Notable structures include numerous private houses, such as his own residence, Hara House, Machida, Tokyo (1973–74). He participated in the 1982 International Competition for the Parc de la Villette, Paris; built the Yamato International Building, Ota-ku, Tokyo (1985–86); the Iida City Museum, Iida, Nagano (1986–88); and the Sotetsu Culture Center, Yokohama, Kanagawa (1988–90). Larger work includes: the Umeda Sky Building, Kita-ku, Osaka (1988–93); the Kyoto JR Railway Station, Sakyo-ku, Kyoto (1990–97); and the more recent Sapporo Dome, where World Cup soccer matches were held (2002).

ORIMOTO HOUSE
UCHIKO
2003

FLOOR AREA: 169 m^2
CLIENT: Private client
COST: not disclosed

Images of the Orimoto House reveal a striking superposition of real and reflected views of the landscape. Set on a 679 m^2 site, this house has a total floor area of 169 m^2. With a main building in the form of a quarter circle, and an annex used as a teahouse, the juncture of the two elements creates a courtyard where glazed façades face each other. Hiroshi Hara explains the literary background of this composition: "It was a few years ago that I designed a junior high school that the Nobel laureate writer Kenzaburo Oe had once attended in a 'valley among a forest in Shikoku Island,' a location where some of his novels take place. The Orimoto House is adjacent to the Ohse Middle School. The valley, which is repeatedly referred to in Oe's texts, is in fact a very narrow strip of land surrounded by mountains and forests reminiscent of old Japanese folktales. Oe has made this valley into a literary space through some 30 'semiotic places.' Ohse Middle School was built using the same method as the literature of Oe. Fictional places from his works were materialized in an attempt to interlace fiction and reality. Now, the Orimoto House is an extension of such mode of planning; two buildings standing face to face and the square courtyard in between imply that each of these elements is a 'symbolized place.' The materialization of a complex 'semiotic field' subject to temporal transformation is the essential concept of the design."

Aufnahmen des Hauses zeigen eine auffallende Überlagerung von realen und gespiegelten Landschaftsansichten. Das Gebäude steht auf einem 679 m^2 großen Grundstück, hat eine Gesamtfläche von 169 m^2 und im Grundriss die Form eines Viertelkreises. Der daneben stehende Anbau wird als Teehaus genutzt. An der Verbindungsstelle ist ein Hof entstanden, der von einander gegenüber liegenden Glasfassaden eingefasst wird. Hara erklärt den literarischen Hintergrund für seine Gestaltung: „Vor einigen Jahren entwarf ich Gebäude für eine Sekundarschule, die einst der Literaturnobelpreisträger Kenzaburo Oe besucht hatte. Sie liegt in einem Tal in einem Wald auf der Insel Shikoku, Schauplatz einiger Romane von Oe. Das Orimoto-Haus steht in der Nähe dieser Schule. Das Tal, das in vielen Büchern Oes beschrieben wird, ist umgeben von Bergen und Wäldern, die an alte japanische Märchen erinnern. Oe hat dieses Tal in einen literarischen Raum verwandelt, indem er dort in seinen Romanen 30 ‚semiotische Orte' ansiedelte. Die Ohse-Schule entstand in ähnlicher Weise: Orte aus seinen Büchern wurden in Gebäude umgesetzt mit dem Versuch, Fiktion und Realität zu verknüpfen. Mit dem Orimoto-Haus haben wir diese Entwurfsidee wieder aufgegriffen. Zwei Häuser stehen sich gegenüber, und der quadratische Hof dazwischen impliziert, dass jedes von ihnen einen ‚symbolisierten Ort' darstellt. Die Materialisierung eines komplexen ‚semiotischen Feldes', das zeitlichen Veränderungen unterworfen ist, das war der zentrale Entwurfsgedanke."

Les photographies de cette maison montrent une superposition surprenante de vues du paysage réelles et réfléchies. Implantée sur un terrain de 679 m^2, sa surface totale s'élève à 169 m^2. Elle se compose d'une partie principale en quart de cercle et d'une annexe faisant office de maison de thé, entre lesquelles s'étend la cour extérieure sur laquelle donnent les façades vitrées des bâtiments. Hiroshi Hara explique ainsi le contexte littéraire de cette composition : « Quelques années auparavant, j'avais conçu un bâtiment pour un collège qu'avait jadis fréquenté le Prix Nobel de littérature Kenzaburo Oe dans une ‹ vallée au milieu d'une forêt de l'île de Shikoku ›, où se déroulent d'ailleurs quelques-uns de ses romans. La maison Orimoto est adjacente à cette école de Ohse. La vallée à laquelle se réfèrent souvent les textes de Oe, est en fait une très étroite bande de terre entourée de montagnes et de forêts qui évoquent les anciennes légendes populaires nippones. Oe en avait fait un espace ‹ littéraire › à travers 30 ‹ lieux sémiotiques ›. » L'École moyenne d'Ohse a été édifiée selon les mêmes méthodes que celles de l'écriture de Oe. Des lieux de fiction inspirés de ses œuvres ont été matérialisés dans une tentative d'entrelacer fiction et réalité. La maison Orimoto est une extension de ce processus de planification. Deux bâtiments se font face et la cour carrée qui les relie impliquant que chacun d'entre eux est un ‹ lieu symbolique ›. La matérialisation d'un ‹ champ sémiotique › complexe sujet à une transformation temporelle est le concept de base de ce projet. »

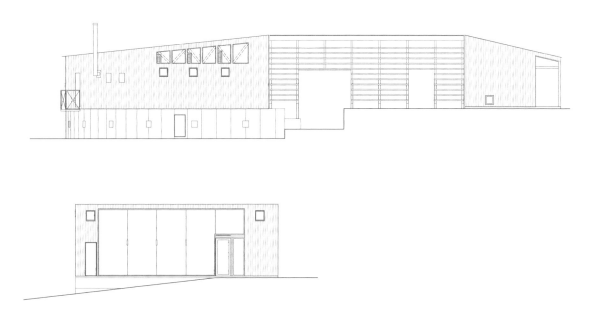

Photographs of the Orimoto House intentionally play on the ambiguity of surfaces and reflections, in the mood of the architect's inspiration, drawn from the literature of Kenzaburo Oe.

Abbildungen des Orimoto-Hauses spielen bewusst mit der Mehrdeutigkeit von Oberflächen und Spiegelungen – ganz im Sinne des Architekten, der sich von Kenzaburo Oes Romanen inspirieren ließ.

Les photographies de la maison Orimoto jouent intentionnellement sur l'ambiguïté des surfaces et des reflets, dans l'esprit de l'inspiration de l'architecte tirée des œuvres de l'écrivain Kenzaburo Oe.

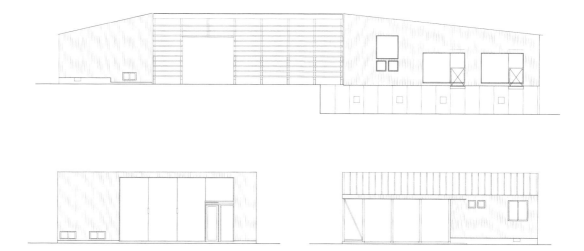

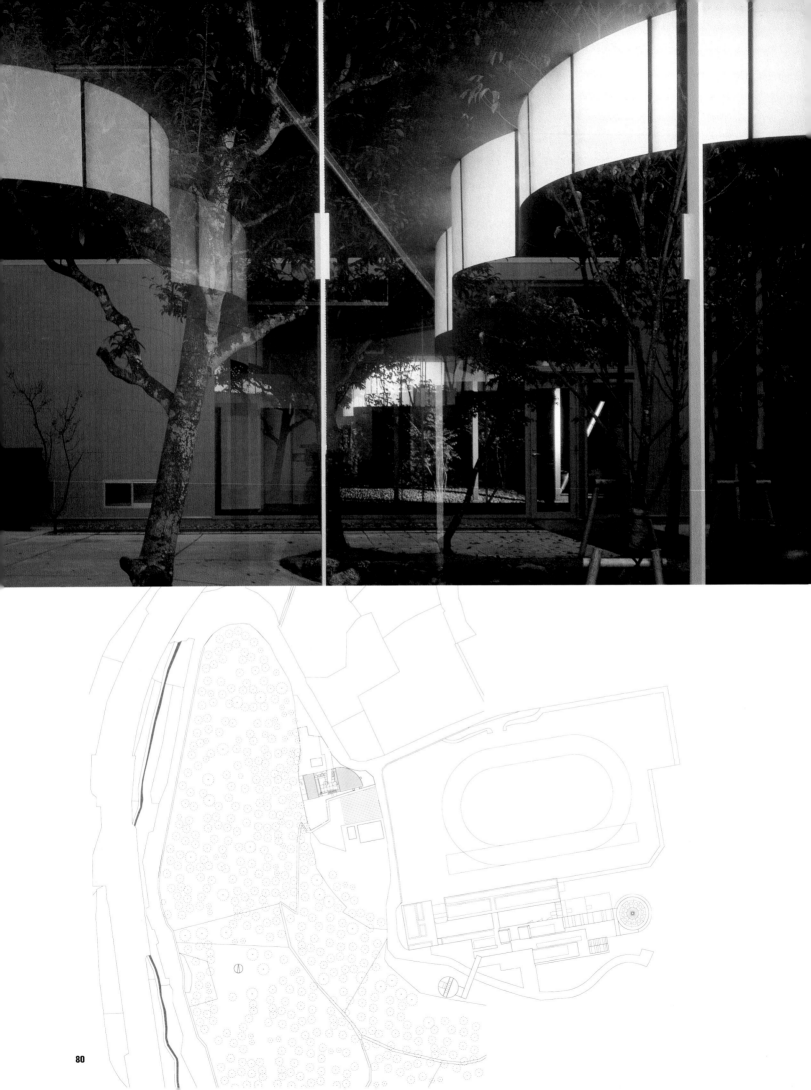

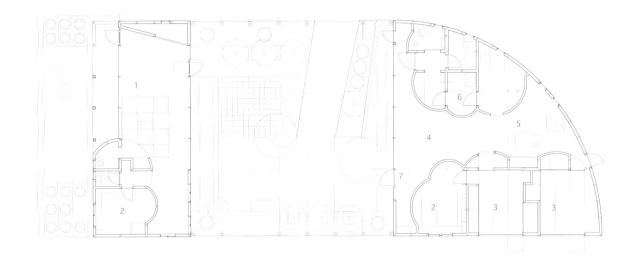

Varying degrees of transparency and opacity characterize the spaces of the Orimoto House, giving it characteristics that are at once modern and quintessentially traditional. Light and space are dissolved in ways that are not typical of Western architecture, for example.

Unterschiedliche Grade von Transparenz und Massivität verleihen den Räumen des Orimoto-Hauses eine moderne und zugleich traditionelle Note. Licht und Raum verschmelzen in einer Art und Weise, die für die westliche Architektur untypisch ist.

La maison Orimoto se caractérise par ses divers degrés de transparence et d'opacité qui lui confèrent un esprit à la fois moderne et fondamentalement traditionnel. La lumière et l'espace se dissolvent d'une façon peu courante dans l'architecture occidentale.

ARATA
ISOZAKI

ARATA ISOZAKI & ASSOCIATES
NOGIZAKA ATELIER
9-6-17, Akasaka
Minato-ku
Tokyo 107-0052

Tel: + 81 3 34 05 15 26
Fax: + 81 3 34 75 52 65
e-mail: info@isozaki.co.jp

Born in Oita City on the Island of Kyushu in 1931, **ARATA ISOZAKI** graduated from the Architectural Faculty of the University of Tokyo in 1954 and established Arata Isozaki & Associates in 1963, having worked in the office Kenzo Tange. Winner of the 1986 Royal Institute of British Architects Gold Medal, he has been a juror of major competitions, such as that held in 1988 for the new Kansai International Airport. Notable buildings include: the Museum of Modern Art, Gunma (1971-74); the Tsukuba Center Building, Tsukuba (1978-83); the Museum of Contemporary Art, Los Angeles (1981-86); the Art Tower Mito, Mito (1986-90); the Team Disney Building, Florida (1990-94); the Center for Japanese Art and Technology, Cracow, Poland (1991-94); B-con Plaza, Oita (1991-95); the Higashi Shizuoka Plaza Cultural Complex, Shizuoka; and the Center of Science and Industry (COSI), Columbus, Ohio. More recently, aside from the Yamaguchi Center for Arts and Media featured here, he has taken on a number of projects in Qatar, including the National Bank, the National Library and the master plan for the Qatar Education City. Isozaki has also received a commission from the Aga Khan to develop the three new campuses of the University of Central Asia to be located in Tekeli, Kazakhstan, Naryn, Kyrgyz Republic, and Khorog, Tajikistan.

YAMAGUCHI CENTER FOR ARTS AND MEDIA
YAMAGUCHI
2001 - 03

FLOOR AREA: 14 824 m²
CLIENT: City of Yamaguchi
COST: $64.5 million

Yamaguchi is the capital city of Yamaguchi Prefecture, Japan. It is the smallest prefectural capital in Japan. In 2003, the city had an estimated population of 142 236. The city was founded on April 10, 1929. Arata Isozaki designed a cultural complex for the city, including a library and three studios. With a total floor area of 14 824 m², the building is quite large. The design provides for foyers and corridors to connect the rooms but also to be used for exhibitions and performances, allowing for unexpected interaction between visitors. A glass box functions as an inner courtyard. One of the remarkable features of the structures is a "unidirectional curved roof with a hybrid structure of arches and suspensions." As Isozaki explains, "This curved roof's main vertical support is Vielendeel-trussed , which also functions as an earthquake-proof device along the transverse axis." Isozaki has designed a number of multifunctional cultural complexes, in Japan, Europe and the United States. As always, he masters the use of space and form in ways that defy clear stylistic classification. The overarching curved roof gives a decidedly contemporary look to the Yamaguchi Center for Arts and Media, while the organization of the interior seeks to innovate on the austerity that is frequently seen in this kind of complex.

Yamaguchi ist die Hauptstadt der gleichnamigen japanischen Präfektur, und dabei die kleinste Präfektur-Hauptstadt in Japan. Sie wurde am 10. April 1929 gegründet und verzeichnete 2003 eine Einwohnerzahl von 142 236. Isozaki entwarf das städtische Kulturzentrum mit Bibliothek und drei Künstlerateliers. Mit seinen 14 824 m² Gesamtfläche ist das Gebäude ziemlich groß. Der Entwurf sah Foyers und Verbindungsgänge vor, die aber auch für Ausstellungen und Aufführungen genutzt werden und zwanglose Begegnungen zwischen den Besuchern ermöglichen sollten. Ein Glaskasten dient als Innenhof. Ein bemerkenswertes Merkmal dieses Gebäudekomplexes ist „ein in einer Richtung geschwungenes Dach mit einer konstruktiven Mischung aus Bogentragwerk und Hängesystem". Isozaki erklärte weiter: „Vierendeel-Träger bilden die vertikalen Hauptstützen des geschwungenen Dachs und dienen auch als erdbebensichere Tragwerksteile entlang der Querachse." Isozaki hat nicht nur in Japan, sondern auch in Europa und den USA multifunktionale Kulturbauten errichtet. Wie stets hat er auch hier die funktionale Raumeinteilung und die Gestaltung der Form in einer Weise gemeistert, die sich jeder klaren stilistischen Klassifizierung entzieht. Das hoch gewölbte Dach verleiht dem Kunst- und Medienzentrum einen entschieden zeitgenössischen Charakter. Im Innern ist der Architekt bewusst von der sonst bei solchen Gebäuden üblichen strengen Einteilung abgewichen und suchte gestalterisch nach neuen Lösungen.

Fondée en 1929, et peuplée de 142 236 habitants, siège de la préfecture éponyme, Yamaguchi est la plus petite des capitales préfectorales du Japon. C'est pour elle qu'Arata Isozaki a conçu un complexe culturel assez vaste de 14 824 m² comprenant une bibliothèque et trois ateliers. Les salles sont connectées par des halls et des corridors mais la possibilité d'expositions et de spectacles a également été prévue, ce qui permet des interactions intéressantes entre les visiteurs. Une boîte de verre sert de cour intérieure. L'une des caractéristiques les plus remarquables de ce bâtiment est sa « toiture unidirectionnelle à structure hybride d'arcs et de suspensions ». Comme l'explique l'architecte : « Le principal support de ce toit incurvé est une poutre de structure Vielendeel qui sert également de dispositif anti-sismique sur l'axe transversal. » Isozaki a déjà conçu un certain nombre de complexes culturels polyvalents aussi bien au Japon qu'en Europe ou aux États-Unis. Comme toujours, il maîtrise l'espace et la forme d'une manière qui échappe à toute classification stylistique. Ce toit en vague confère à ce centre une allure décidément contemporaine, tandis que son organisation intérieure innove par rapport aux plans habituels beaucoup plus stricts de ce type d'équipement culturel.

Isozaki has considerable experience in the design and construction of buildings intended for the arts. His theater (above) is at once strictly delineated and crisply executed. He has also long been interested in contrasts between light and dark, such as those visible in the night view (above left).

Isozaki verfügt über einen reichen Erfahrungsschatz, was den Entwurf und die Realisierung von Kulturbauten angeht. Sein Theatergebäude (oben) ist in Entwurf und Ausführung gleichermaßen klar und präzise. Isozaki beschäftigt sich seit langem auch mit Hell-Dunkel-Kontrasten – was die Nachtansicht (oben links) verrät.

Isozaki possède une grande expérience de la conception et de la construction de bâtiments destinés aux activités artistiques. Son théâtre (ci-dessus) est dessiné et réalisé avec la même précision. L'architecte s'intéresse aussi depuis longtemps aux contrastes entre l'ombre et la lumière, comme on le voit dans cette vue nocturne (en haut à gauche).

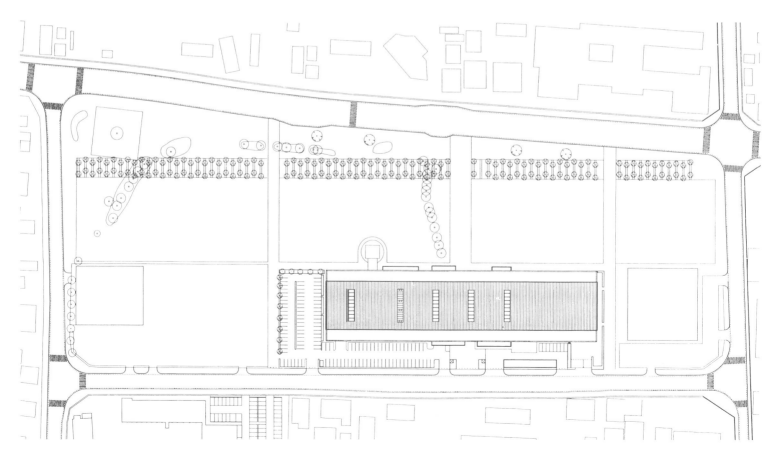

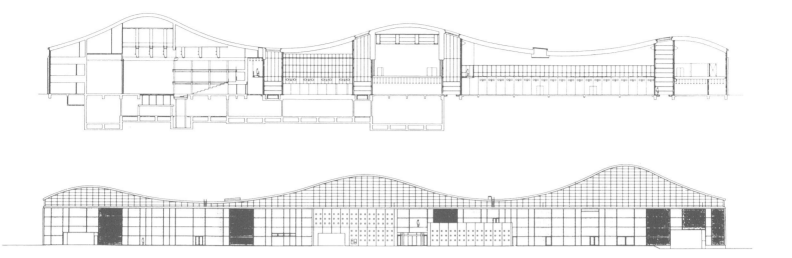

Elevation and section show the rolling hill-like design of the roof, enclosing a variety of different functions and generating such powerful spaces as the lobby (below), with its asymmetrical curved roof.

Aufriss und Schnitt zeigen das stark geschwungene Profil des Daches, unter dem verschiedene Funktionsbereiche versammelt sind, darunter so eindrucksvolle Räume wie das Foyer (unten) mit seiner asymmetrisch gewölbten Decke.

La coupe et l'élévation montrent le toit en vallonnement qui recouvre toute diversité de fonctions et génère des volumes puissants, dont le hall d'entrée à couverture incurvée asymétrique.

TOYO
ITO

TOYO ITO & ASSOCIATES
1-19-4, Shibuya
Shibuya-ku,
Tokyo 150-0002
Tel: + 81 3 34 09 58 22
Fax: + 81 3 34 09 59 69

TOYO ITO & ASSOCIATES
Fujiya Building
19-4 1-Chome, Shibuya
Shibuya-ku,
Tokyo 150-0002
Tel: + 81 3 34 09 58 22
Fax: + 81 3 34 09 59 69

Born in 1941 in Seoul, Korea, **TOYO ITO** graduated from the University of Tokyo in 1965, and worked in the office of Kiyonori Kikutake until 1969. He created his own office, Urban Robot (URBOT), in Tokyo in 1971, assuming the name of Toyo Ito & Associates in 1979. His completed work includes: the Silver Hut residence, Tokyo (1984); the Tower of the Winds, Yokohama, Kanagawa (1986); the Yatsushiro Municipal Museum, Yatsushiro, Kumamoto (1989–91); and the Elderly People's Home (1992–94) and Fire Station (1992–95), both also located in Yatsushiro on the island of Kyushu. He participated in the Shanghai Luijiazui Center Area International Planning and Urban Design Consultation in 1992, and has built a Public Kindergarten in Eckenheim, Frankfurt, Germany (1988–91). Recent projects include his Odate Jukai Dome Park, Odate (1995–97); the Nagaoka Lyric Hall, Nagaoka, Niigata (1995–97) and the Ota-ku Resort Complex, Tobu-cho, Chiisagata-gun, Nagano (1996–98). One of his most successful and widely published projects, the Médiathèque in Sendai, was completed in 2001. He designed a temporary pavilion for the Serpentine Gallery in London (2002). He was awarded the Golden Lion for Lifetime Achievement of the 8th International Venice Architecture Biennale the same year.

TOD'S OMOTESANDO BUILDING
TOKYO
2002·04

FLOOR AREA: 2550 m²
CLIENT: Holpaf B. V.
COST: not disclosed

Set on Omotesando Avenue, quite close to the Dior building by Kazuyo Sejima, Tod's has a total floor area of 2550 m². The actual retail sales area occupies 450 m² on the first and second floors, while the third to fifth floors are used as offices, the sixth floor as an event space and the seventh for a private dining room, meeting room, and roof garden. Toyo Ito, normally quite reserved, has said, "The Tod's Omotesando Building is an ambitious project embodying concepts and techniques at the forefront of contemporary architecture. With this project, I am striving to transcend the architectural Modernism that characterized the twentieth century." The unusual concrete and glass façade was generated by superimposing the silhouettes of nine zelkova trees, although this biological origin may not be readily evident to passersby. Because of its L-shaped plan, the structure actually has six façades and not four, each of them designed in the same way. Ito compares the changing nature of the building as it rises to the differences in trees from base to top. He also renders explicit the fact that experience he gained with the Sendai Médiathèque or the Serpentine Pavilion in London has had a direct influence on this outstanding and unusual building

Das an der Omotesando Avenue unweit des Dior-Hauses von Kazuyo Sejima gelegene Geschäftshaus Tod's hat eine Gesamtgeschossfläche von 2550 m². Die 450 m² Verkaufsflächen befinden sich im Erdgeschoss und ersten Obergeschoss; Büros sind im dritten bis fünften Stockwerk untergebracht; die sechste Etage ist Veranstaltungen vorbehalten und im siebten befinden sich ein Raum für Geschäftsessen, ein Konferenzraum und ein Dachgarten. Über dieses Projekt sagt der normalerweise recht reservierte Architekt: „Das Tod's-Gebäude Omotesando ist ein ehrgeiziges Projekt; es verkörpert Konzepte und Techniken an vorderster Front der zeitgenössischen Architektur. Mit diesem Entwurf versuche ich, die Archi-

tekturmoderne des 20. Jahrhunderts zu transzendieren." Die ungewöhnliche Beton-und-Glasfassade entstand durch Überlagerung der Silhouetten von neun Zelkova-Bäumen, wobei dieser botanische Bezug wohl den wenigsten Passanten auffällt. Aufgrund seiner L-Form hat der Bau sechs Fassaden statt nur vier – alle identisch gestaltet. Ito vergleicht das sich nach oben verändernde Erscheinungsbild des Gebäudes mit dem Unterschied zwischen Baumstamm und Baumkrone und erklärt ausdrücklich, dass die Erfahrungen, die er beim Entwurf und Bau der Mediathek in Sendai und dem Pavillon der Londoner Serpentine Gallery machte, direkt in dieses herausragende und ungewöhnliche Gebäude eingeflossen sind.

Sur l'avenue Omotesando, assez près de l'immeuble Dior de Kazuyo Sejima, celui de Tod's mesure 2550 m², dont 450 pour la vente en au rez-de-chaussée et au premier étage. Les trois étages suivants sont consacrés aux bureaux, le sixième à un espace pour manifestations, le septième à une salle à manger privée, une salle de conférence et un jardin. Toyo Ito, généralement assez réservé, a déclaré : « Le Tod's Omotesando Building est un ambitieux projet qui incarne des concepts et des techniques à l'avant-garde de l'architecture contemporaine ... Je m'efforce de transcender le modernisme architectural qui a caractérisé le XXe siècle. » L'étonnante façade en verre et en béton est issue de la superposition des silhouettes de neuf zelkovas (arbres), bien que cette origine végétale ne soit pas évidente pour le passant. Du fait de son plan en L, le bâtiment possède six façades, chacune conçue de la même façon. Ito compare la transformation des façades au fur et à mesure qu'elles s'élèvent aux différences qui marquent la silhouette d'un arbre, de ses racines à son couronnement. Il reconnaît également que l'expérience acquise lors de la construction de la Médiathèque de Sendai ou du Pavillon de la Serpentine à Londres a directement influencé ce remarquable projet.

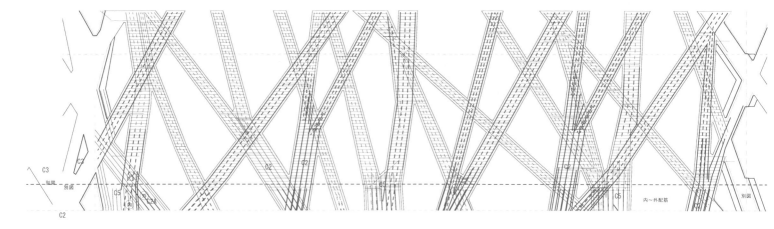

Located almost at the center of the fashionable Omotesando-Avenue in Tokyo, the unusual branch-like façade of the Tod's building stands out from its more traditional neighbors. Floor levels are only apparent with the transparency of the structure, and not at all through delineation on the façade.

Fast genau in der Mitte der eleganten Omotesando Avenue in Tokio gelegen, ragt das Gebäude mit seiner ungewöhnlichen, an das Astwerk von Bäumen erinnernden Fassadengestaltung aus der Masse seiner konventionelleren Nachbarn hervor. Die einzelnen Geschosse sind von außen lediglich durch die Transparenz der Fassade zu erkennen und nicht durch Gliederung an der Außenfläche.

Situé presque au centre de l'élégant quartier de l'avenue Omotesando à Tokyo, la façade « à branches » de l'immeuble Tod's se distingue de ses voisins beaucoup plus traditionnels. C'est la transparence qui laisse percevoir la délimitation des niveaux et non la structure extérieure.

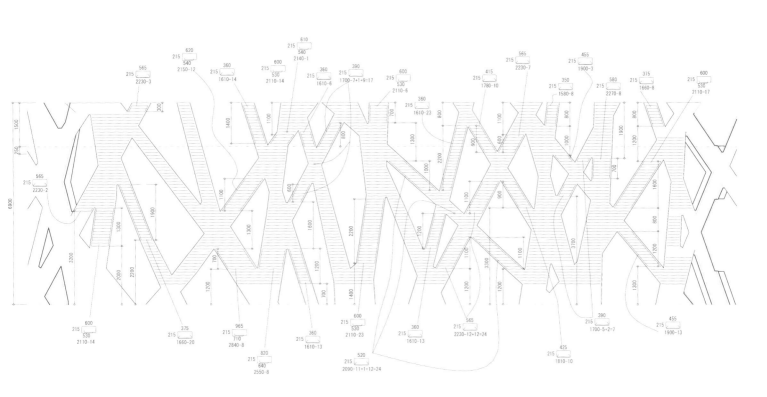

Toyo Ito was not responsible for most of the interior décor of the Tod's shop, but his façades and stairway nonetheless set the tone for the whole building. A folded paper with the branching design of the façade (right) shows how the overall design was developed.

Die Innenausstattung stammt zwar zum größten Teil nicht von Toyo Ito, sein Fassaden- und Treppenentwurf hat aber dennoch das ganze Gebäude entscheidend geprägt. Ein Faltpapier mit der sich baumähnlich verzweigenden Fassadenstruktur (rechts) dokumentiert die Entwicklung des Projektes.

Si Toyo Ito n'a pas été chargé de l'aménagement intérieur de l'immeuble, ses façades et son escalier ont évidemment donné le ton à l'ensemble. Un papier plié reproduisant la façade à branches montre un état de la mise au point du projet (à droite).

From its upper levels, particularly the seventh floor meeting room (left), the Tod's building offers a spectacular view of Tokyo, particularly since there are few tall structures in the Omotesando district. The strong, irregular branching design of the façade permitted the architect to avoid the use of interior columns (right).

Die oberen Etagen des Gebäudes, besonders der Konferenzraum im siebten Stock (links), bieten fantastische Ausblicke über die Stadt Tokio, vor allem deshalb, weil es im Omotesando-Bezirk nur wenige Hochhäuser gibt. Die unregelmäßig verästelte Fassadenkonstruktion ermöglichte es dem Architekten, auf Stützen im Innern zu verzichten (rechts).

De ses derniers étages, en particulier de la salle de réunion du 7e niveau (à gauche) l'immeuble Tod's offre une vue spectaculaire sur Tokyo, d'autant plus que les autres constructions du quartier sont généralement peu élevées. La façade structurelle en branches a permis à l'architecte d'éviter toute colonne intérieure (à droite).

B1F plan

1F plan

2F plan

3F plan

4F plan

5F plan

6F plan

7F plan

I-PROJECT
FUKUOKA
2003-05

FLOOR AREA: 5162 m²
CLIENT: Fukuoka City
COST: $12.4 million

The city of Fukuoka began in 1994 to create an artificial island on the eastern side of Hakata Bay. A 15-hectare section of the island, half of which had been completed by 2004, is to be a park. Working with the landscape architects Sohgoh Landscape Planning Office, Toyo Ito imagined a series of "topographical undulations" whose core is a 5162 m² facility, including three greenhouses intended as rest areas for reading or eating. Though its undulating roof may bring to mind Renzo Piano's Paul Klee Center in Bern, the forms of Ito's structure appear much freer. As the architect explains, "A unique design method called 'Shape Analysis by Optimization' was utilized in order to create optimal shapes as incremental alterations. Computer simulations were used to study bending stress, deforming the original forms as little as possible. Repeating and advancing from this architectural and structural design process, a free-form reinforced concrete shell structure with 400 mm thickness is created." The entire roof is planted and a pedestrian path along the roof deck links interior and exterior spaces. The completion of the complex was keyed to the National Urban Greenery Fukuoka Fair, for which the building was used as a "theme hall" in the fall of 2005.

1994 begann die Stadt Fukuoka, auf der Ostseite der Hakata-Bucht eine künstliche Insel aufzuschütten. 15 ha der Insel, die 2004 zur Hälfte fertig gestellt war, sollten als Park angelegt werden. In Zusammenarbeit mit den Landschaftsplanern vom Büro Sohgoh konzipierte Toyo Ito eine Reihe „topografischer Ondulationen" mit einem 5162 m² großen „Kern" aus Besuchereinrichtungen und drei Gewächshäusern, in denen man sich ausruhen, picknicken oder lesen kann. Das wellenförmige Dach erinnert ein wenig an Renzo Pianos Zentrum Paul Klee in Bern, Itos Bau wirkt formal aber wesentlich freier. Zu dem Entwurfsprozess äußerte sich der Architekt: „Um optimale Formen erhalten und ihre schrittweise Veränderrung untersuchen zu können, wurde eine einzigartige Entwurfstechnik - genannt ‚Shape Analysis by Optimization' (Formanalyse durch Optimierung) -

angewandt. Wir nutzten Computersimulationen zur Analyse von Krümmungsbeanspruchungen, um die Deformation der Ausgangsformen so gering wie möglich zu halten. So entstand in diesem architektonischen und tragwerksplanerischen Entwurfsprozess durch Wiederholung und Ableitung eine plastisch geformte, 40 cm dicke Stahlbetonschalenkonstruktion." Das gesamte Dach ist begrünt; ein Fußweg führt darüber hinweg und verbindet den Innen- mit dem Außenraum. Der Komplex wurde rechtzeitig zur „Nationalen Stadtgrünmesse" von Fukuoka im Herbst 2005 fertig und als „Themenhalle" genutzt.

En 1994, la ville de Fukuoka a entamé les travaux d'aménagement d'une île artificielle sur la rive orientale de la baie d'Hakata. 15 hectares doivent devenir un parc dont la moitié était aménagée en 2004. En collaboration avec les architectes paysagistes du Sohgoh Landscape Planning Office, Toyo Ito a imaginé une série « d'ondulations topographiques » dont le noyau est un bâtiment de 5162 m² comprenant trois serres qui sont des lieux de repos pour lire ou se restaurer. Si ces formes peuvent rappeler le centre Paul Klee de Renzo Piano à Berne, les formes japonaises semblent beaucoup plus libres. Comme l'explique l'architecte : « Une méthode de conception spéciale appelée ‹ analyse de forme par optimisation › a été utilisée pour créer ces formes optimisées par modifications incrémentales. Des simulations par ordinateur ont permis d'étudier les contraintes de fléchissement pour réduire au maximum la déformation des formes d'origine. Par un processus de répétition et d'avancement progressif ... nous avons créé une structure de coque en béton de forme libre de 40 cm d'épaisseur. » La totalité du toit est végétalisée et un cheminement pour piétons le long de la terrasse en toiture relie les espaces extérieurs et intérieurs. L'achèvement de ce complexe a accompagné l'ouverture du Salon national d'espaces verts urbains de Fukuoka où il a servi de « hall thématique » à l'automne 2005.

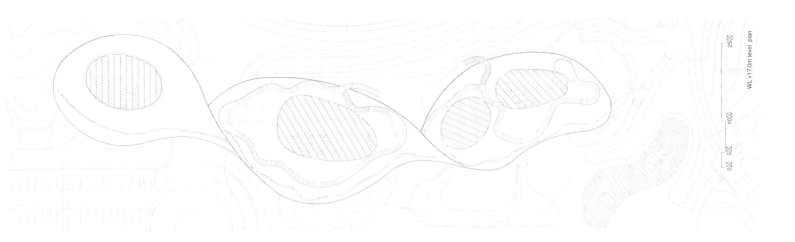

WL +17.0m level plan

The amoeboid plan and grass-covered roofs of the complex certainly give it a biomorphic appearance, even if no specific organism is at the origin of the design. Although flowing curves are typical of Toyo Ito's architecture, this building seems to be unrelated to almost any particular stylistic current.

Der amöbenartige Grundriss und die Gras-dächer sind für das biomorphe Erscheinungs-bild des Gebäudekomplexes verantwortlich. Trotz der Schwünge und Kurven, die typisch sind für Toyo Itos Architektur, lässt sich dieses Gebäude keiner bestimmten stilistischen Strömung zuordnen.

Le plan amibien et les toits recouverts de gazon de ce complexe lui donnent un aspect biomorphique, sans référence cependant avec un organisme spécifique. Bien que les courbes soient typiques des réalisations de Toyo Ito, ce bâtiment semble à l'écart de tout courant stylistique précis.

10

WARO KISHI

WARO KISHI + K.ASSOCIATES/ ARCHITECTS

4F Yutaka Building.
366 Karigane-cho
Nakagyo-ku
Kyoto, 604-8115 Japan

Tel: + 81 7 52 13 02 58
Fax: + 81 7 52 13 02 59
e-mail: kishi@k-associates.com
Web: www.k-associates.com

Born in Yokohama in 1950, **WARO KISHI** graduated from the Department of Electronics at Kyoto University in 1973, and from the Department of Architecture of the same institution two years later. He completed his postgraduate studies in Kyoto in 1978, and worked in the office of Masayuki Kurokawa in Tokyo from 1978 to 1981. He created Waro Kishi + K.Associates/ Architects in Kyoto in 1993. His completed works include: the Autolab automobile showroom, Kyoto (1989); the Kyoto-Kagaku Research Institute, Kizu-cho, Kyoto (1990); the Yunokabashi Bridge, Ashikita-cho, Kumamoto (1991); Other SD Office, Sono-becho, Funai-gun, Kyoto (1993); as well as numerous private houses. Recent work includes: the Memorial Hall, Ube, Yamaguchi (1997); a house in Higashi-nada, Kobe (1997); and a House in Suzaku, Nara (1997-98). More recently, he designed the House in Fukaya, Saitama (2000), and House II in Kurakuen, Nishinomiya, Hyogo (2001).

LUNA DI MIELE OMOTESANDO BUILDING

TOKYO 2004

FLOOR AREA: 108 m²
CLIENT: Private client
COST: not disclosed

With a tiny footprint of just 24 m² on a 31 m² site, this design houses a jeweler's shop and office in a five-story, steel-frame and reinforced-concrete building. The total floor area is 108 m², with the store on the first four floors and a public relations area and customer service office on the top floor. Each floor comprises a single space with a stairway. Waro Kishi says, "My two basic design ideas were to adopt a structural system without columns in order to make effective use of the limited area and to make the overall structure as lightweight as possible in order to simplify the foundation ... Grey pane glass, transparent glass and stainless mesh are layered on the façade of this urban building. The surface has the smoothness of glass but also the semblance of depth. Lighting installed between the overlapping materials gives the building a completely different look at night. This is an extremely small building, but I wanted it to be a delightful, jewel-like addition to the Tokyo townscape." Particularly in a chic area like Omotesando, land is extremely difficult to come by and very expensive. It is thus incumbent on the architect to be extremely careful that there is no wasted space. Kishi's precision and clever design fulfill these requirements.

Dieses Stahlrahmen- und Stahlbetonhaus mit seiner sehr kleinen Grundfläche von nur 24 m² auf einem kaum größeren Grundstück von 31 m² enthält auf fünf Stockwerken den Laden und das Büro eines Juweliers. Die Gesamtgeschossfläche beträgt 108 m². Die Verkaufsräume nehmen die ersten vier Stockwerke ein, das Büro befindet sich auf der obersten Etage. Jedes Geschoss besteht aus einem einzigen Raum, alle sind durch eine Treppe verbunden. Kishi erklärt: „Meine zwei Grundgedanken waren erstens eine stützenfreie Konstruktion, um den begrenzt zur Verfügung stehenden Raum voll zu nutzen, und zweitens ein möglichst leichter Bau, um die Fundamentierung zu vereinfachen. Die mehrlagige Fassade besteht aus grau getönten Fensterscheiben, Klarglas und Stahlmaschendraht. Die Oberfläche ist daher so glatt wie Glas, besitzt aber auch optische Tiefe. In die Lagen der Fassade integrierte Beleuchtungskörper lassen den Bau nachts buchstäblich in einem ganz anderen Licht erscheinen. Dies ist ein extrem schmales Gebäude, aber ich wollte daraus eine entzückende, juwelartige Bereicherung der Tokioter Stadtlandschaft machen." Vor allem in einem Nobelviertel wie Omotesando sind Grundstücke schwer zu haben und extrem teuer. Ein Architekt muss hier also darauf achten, dass kein Raum verschenkt wird. Mit Präzision und cleverer Gestaltung hat Kishi diese Bedingung erfüllt.

Pour une emprise au sol d'à peine 24 m² sur une parcelle de 31 m², ce petit immeuble de cinq niveaux à ossature en acier et béton armé accueille une boutique de bijoutier et un bureau. La surface totale utile est de 108 m². La boutique occupe les quatre premiers niveaux, le service client et un bureau de relations publiques le dernier étage. Chaque niveau comprend une pièce unique et la cage d'escalier. Pour Waro Kishi : « Mes deux idées étaient d'adopter un système structurel qui évite toute colonne afin d'utiliser au maximum les surfaces disponibles et de rendre l'ensemble aussi léger que possible pour simplifier le problème des fondations ... Des panneaux de verre gris, d'autres de verre transparent et une résille en acier inoxydable recouvrent la façade en superposition. La surface extérieure offre l'aspect doux et lisse du verre, mais donne également une impression de profondeur. L'éclairage entre les superpositions de matériaux confère à cet immeuble un aspect nocturne totalement différent. C'est un immeuble minuscule, mais je voulais cependant qu'il soit comme un bijou raffiné dans le contexte urbain de Tokyo. » Dans un quartier aussi à la mode qu'Omotesando, les terrains sont extrêmement difficiles à trouver et d'un prix très élevé. Il convient donc aux architectes d'être prudents et de ne pas gaspiller l'espace, ce à quoi ont répondu la précision et l'intelligence du projet de Kishi.

Waro Kishi, like other Japanese architects, has developed a particularly advanced design sense when it comes to small urban projects. This building is tiny and yet it shows a high degree of architectural sophistication. Drawings below reveal the assembly process.

Wie andere japanische Architekten hat auch Waro Kishi für kleine städtische Bauprojekte eine besondere gestalterische Sensibilität entwickelt. Dieses Gebäude ist winzig und dennoch ein Stück äußerst raffinierter Architektur. Die Zeichnungen (unten) dokumentieren den Montageprozess.

Comme d'autres architectes japonais, Waro Kishi a développé un sens particulièrement avancé de la conception de petits projets urbains. Cet immeuble de très faibles dimensions témoigne néanmoins d'un haut niveau de sophistication. Le dessin ci-dessous illustre son processus d'assemblage.

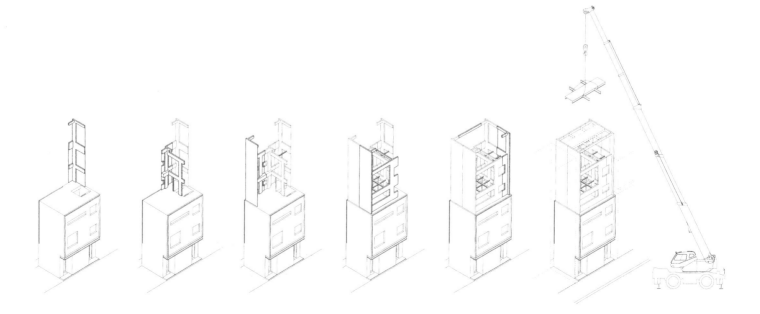

HOUSE IN YOYOGI-UEHARA
TOKYO 2004·05

FLOOR AREA: 119 m²
CLIENT: Private client
COST: not disclosed

This is a single-family house intended for an older couple. Kishi points out that local zoning restrictions and the nature of the site essentially formed the architecture in this case. One difficulty is the slope of the land, that is, that the ground level is one meter higher than the level of the streets on the west and south sides. On a site measuring 85 m², the building, covers 51 m² for a total floor area of 119 m² spread on three floors and a basement. The architect explains that "The overall organization of the building was deliberately made ambiguous. The building is made up of a number of overlapping volumes, including that of the retaining wall, that is, the site itself. Diverse materials are scattered over the building, including concrete, glass mosaic tiles, galbarium steel plate, bronze pane glass, transparent glass and plaster ... Basically the interior is one continuous space, but only a fragment of that space is visible at any one time. The interior has been designed as a mazelike space. Although one can hear the voices and sense the presence of the residents from anywhere in this house, they are, as often as not, hidden from view." It is an interesting measure of Japan's relationship with contemporary architecture to note that an elderly couple could be comfortable with such a modern house.

Dieses Haus baute Kishi für ein älteres Ehepaar. Er wies darauf hin, dass die architektonische Gestaltung in diesem Fall maßgeblich durch die restriktiven Auflagen des lokalen Flächennutzungsplans und die Beschaffenheit des Grundstücks bestimmt wurde. Ein Problem war die Hanglage, so dass das Erdgeschoss einen Meter höher liegen musste als das Straßenniveau auf der West- und der Südseite. Das Grundstück ist 85 m² groß, das Haus überbaut davon 51 m² und hat eine Gesamtfläche von 119 m² über vier Geschosse, inklusive Keller. Der Architekt erklärte dazu: „Die Innengliederung ist absichtlich mehrdeutig. Das Haus besteht aus einer Reihe sich überlagernder Massen einschließlich der Stützmauer des Terrassengrundstücks. Im ganzen Haus sind verschiedene Materialien verwendet,

darunter Beton, Glasmosaiksteinchen, Galbarium-Stahlplatten, bronzefarben getönte Fensterscheiben, Klarglas und Putz ... Das Hausinnere besteht praktisch nur aus einem Raum, der aber nie als Ganzes wahrgenommen wird. Das Innere ist wie ein Labyrinth konzipiert. Obwohl man die Stimmen oder Geräusche von anderen Personen im Haus hören kann, sieht man sie häufig nicht." Der Umstand, dass ein älteres Ehepaar sich offenbar in einem derart modernen Haus wohl fühlt, ist ein interessanter Hinweis auf die Beziehung der Japaner zur zeitgenössischen Architektur.

Cette maison individuelle a été construite pour un couple âgé. Kishi fait remarquer que la réglementation de zonage et la nature du terrain expliquent pour l'essentiel l'architecture de ce projet. Une des difficultés était l'inclinaison du sol qui fait que le rez-de-chaussée est à un mètre au-dessus du niveau des rues sur les côtés ouest et sud. La maison occupe 51 m² d'une parcelle de 85 m² pour une surface utile totale de 119 m² répartie sur trois niveaux et un sous-sol. L'architecte explique que « l'organisation générale de la construction a été délibérément rendue ambiguë. Le bâtiment se compose d'un certain nombre de volumes imbriqués dont celui du mur de soutènement, c'est-à-dire le terrain lui-même. Divers matériaux ont été utilisés dans l'ensemble du projet dont du béton, une mosaïque en carreaux de verre ; des tôles d'acier galbarium (à haute résistance à la corrosion), des panneaux de verre bronze ou transparent et du plâtre ... Fondamentalement, l'intérieur est un espace continu unique dont seule une partie est visible à un instant donné. L'intérieur a été conçu comme une sorte de labyrinthe. Bien que l'on puisse entendre les voix et sentir la présence des résidents de toutes les parties de la maison, on ne les voit pas la plupart du temps ». Qu'un couple d'un certain âge se sente à l'aise dans une maison aussi moderne illustre la relation des Japonais avec l'architecture contemporaine.

A masterly orchestration of volumes and colors gives a sculptural appearance and variety to the exterior and interior spaces of the house.

Die meisterhafte Orchestrierung von Volumen und Farben verleiht diesem Haus innen wie außen den Anschein einer vielgestaltigen Skulptur.

Une orchestration magistrale des volumes et des couleurs donne un aspect sculptural et varié aux volumes intérieurs et extérieurs de la maison.

11

KENGO KUMA

KENGO KUMA & ASSOCIATES
2-24-8, Minamiaoyama
Minato-ku
Tokyo 107-0062

Tel: + 81 3 34 01 77 21
Fax: + 81 3 34 01 77 78
e-mail: kuma@ba2.so-net.ne.jp
Web: www.kkaa.co.jp

Born in 1954 in Kanagawa, **KENGO KUMA** graduated in 1979 from the University of Tokyo, with a Master's degree in Architecture. In 1985–86, he received an Asian Cultural Council Fellowship Grant and was a Visiting Scholar at Columbia University. In 1987, he established the Spatial Design Studio and, in 1991, he created Kengo Kuma & Associates. His work includes: the Gunma Toyota Car Show Room, Maebashi (1989); the Maiton Resort Complex, Phuket, Thailand; Rustic, Office Building, Tokyo; Doric, Office Building, Tokyo; M2, Headquarters for Mazda New Design Team, Tokyo (all in 1991); the Kinjo Golf Club, Club House, Okayama (1992); the Kiro-san Observatory, Ehime (1994); the Atami Guest House, Guest House for Bandai Corp, Atami (1992–95); the Karuizawa Resort Hotel, Karuizawa (1993); the Tomioka Lakewood Golf Club House, Tomioka (1993–96); the Toyoma Noh-Theater, Miyagi (1995–96); and the Japanese Pavilion for the Venice Biennale, Italy (1995). He has also completed the Stone Museum in Nasu, Tochigi, and the Museum of Ando Hiroshige in Batou, Nasu-gun, Tochigi. More recently, he finished the Nagasaki Prefecture Art Museum (March 2005); the Fukusaki Hanging Garden (January 2005); LVMH Osaka (2004); One Omotesando, Tokyo (2003); and the Great (Bamboo) Wall guesthouse, Beijing (2002).

FUKUSAKI HANGING GARDEN
OSAKA
2002-05

FLOOR AREA: 982 m²
CLIENT: Sugimura Warehouse
COST: $850 000

This project is located near the seaside of Osaka and was designed to be a temporary three-dimensional playground for children. Perhaps making reference to the vinyl curtains used in warehouses and factories, Kengo Kuma chose them because of their softness. "Inspired by playing children," he says, "I wanted to create the building with soft and gentle materials. In addition vinyl curtains are not like walls or doors, the whole curtain side can serve as entrance. If people want to enter the indoor space, they can just slash through the part of vinyl curtains. Up to now buildings have been structured by walls and doors and windows. However, the use of vinyl curtains means increasing possibilities for new types of buildings. I felt that this character of a new wall and children's free and fragile forms suit each other." The bright color of the building is also a factor in making it a cheerful place. Preoccupied like many Japanese architects by the fundamental ambiguity of space, Kengo Kuma finds a new solution to the difficult equation linking interior and exterior in architecture. Essentially open space, the Hanging Garden was built on a 2450 m² site. The building covers 552 m² and has a total floor area of 982 m² and a maximum height of 6,96 m.

Dieses Projekt am Meer sollte ursprünglich nur ein temporäres Kinderspielhaus sein. Angeregt von den in Lagerhäusern und Fabriken verwendeten Vinylraumteilern beschloss Kuma, es mit diesen weichen, flexiblen Materialien zu realisieren. „Von spielenden Kindern inspiriert," erklärt er, „wollte ich ein Gebäude aus weichen, nachgiebigen Materialien schaffen. Vinylvorhänge sind anders als feste Wände oder Türen, der ganze Vorhang kann als Eingang dienen. Wenn man den Innenraum betreten will, kann man ihn einfach teilen und hindurchgehen. Bislang hat man Häuser mit Wänden, Türen und Fenstern gebaut. Mit Vinylvorhängen lassen sich neue Bautypen schaffen. Ich fand, dass diese neue Art von ‚Wänden' zu

Kindern passt, die ja ebenfalls frei und fragil sind." Die leuchtende Farbe des Spielhauses trägt ebenfalls dazu bei, es zu einem freundlichen Ort zu machen. Wie viele japanische Architekten beschäftigt sich auch Kuma mit der grundlegenden Mehrdeutigkeit von Raum und hat hier eine neue Lösung der schwierigen architektonischen Aufgabe gefunden, den Innen- mit dem Außenraum zu verbinden. Der „Hängende Garten" – im Wesentlichen ein offener, maximal 6,96 m hoher Raum mit einer Grundfläche von 552 m² und einer Gesamtfläche von 982 m² – steht auf einem 2450 m² großen Grundstück.

Ce terrain de jeux provisoire en trois dimensions, destiné aux enfants, se trouve à Osaka, non loin de la côte. Pensant peut-être aux rideaux de vinyle utilisés dans les entrepôts ou les usines, Kengo Kuma les a choisis uniquement pour leur douceur. « Inspiré par les enfants jouant, je voulais créer un bâtiment à partir de matériaux doux et inoffensifs. De plus, les rideaux en vinyle ne sont pas comme des murs ou des portes ; tout le côté fermé par un rideau peut devenir un accès. Si l'on veut entrer, il suffit d'écarter une partie du rideau. Jusqu'à maintenant les bâtiments se structuraient par des murs, des portes et des fenêtres. L'utilisation de ces rideaux offre de nouvelles possibilités de construction pour de nouveaux types de bâtiments. J'ai pensé que ce nouveau type de mur et les formes fragiles et malléables des enfants pouvaient agréablement cohabiter. » La couleur vive du bâtiment renforce le caractère joyeux du lieu. Préoccupé comme beaucoup d'architectes japonais par l'ambiguïté fondamentale de l'espace, Kengo Kuma a ici trouvé ici une nouvelle solution à l'équation délicate entre l'intérieur et l'extérieur en architecture. Espace essentiellement ouvert, ce « Jardin suspendu » a été construit sur un terrain de 2450 m². Le bâtiment représente une emprise au sol de 552 m² et une surface utile de 982 m² pour une hauteur maximum de 6,96 m.

Working with light materials and bright color, Kengo Kuma shows his capacity to create a unique project that is unlike most of his other work and fits the circumstances.

Kengo Kuma arbeitet mit leichten Materialien sowie leuchtenden Farben und stellt so seine Fähigkeit unter Beweis, an die jeweiligen Gegebenheiten angepasste Einzellösungen zu finden.

Travaillant avec des matériaux légers et des couleurs vives, Kengo Kuma montre sa capacité à créer un projet de caractère unique mais adapté aux contraintes.

The use of vinyl strip curtains encourages a sense of play and discovery in the building intended for use by children.

Vorhänge aus Vinylbändern betonen das Spielerische der Konstruktion, in der Kinder ihre Entdeckerfreude ausleben können.

L'utilisation de rideaux en bandes de vinyle stimule le goût du jeu et de la découverte chez les enfants auxquels ces installations sont destinées.

NAGASAKI PREFECTURE ART MUSEUM
NAGASAKI 2003 - 05

FLOOR AREA: 9898 m²
CLIENT: Nagasaki Prefecture
COST: $45 million

As Kengo Kuma explains, the fact that Nagasaki was the only port permitted to remain open while Japan was closed to the rest of the world, it boasts a substantial collection of Spanish and Portuguese works of art. The 12 679 m² site had the particularity of having a canal run through it. Kuma explains that "To make the canal one with the art museum, I created an intermediate space along the canal, and made it a promenade for city residents and a place for appreciating works of art. This space was protected from the strong sun by stone louvers that created a breezy, pleasant shade." A "box-shaped" glass bridge crosses the canal, making it visible to all the visitors of the museum. The roof of the structure is also used as a gallery space with a view of the city's port. With a footprint of 6248 m² and a floor area of 9898 m² this is a large structure, handled with the typical subtlety and intelligence that the architect always demonstrates. Kengo Kuma is also quite outspoken about certain aspects of the design. As he says, "In Nagasaki, I developed a new supporting detail for stone louvers using solid steel columns. Nagasaki, located in southern Japan, is known for its Colonial-style veranda architecture using wooden latticework. The detail I used here is a contemporary version of this traditional architecture; it also is a criticism of contemporary Japanese architecture that ignores both indigenous climate and landscape."

Die Tatsache, dass Nagasaki der einzige offene Hafen war, als sich Japan gegenüber dem Rest der Welt verschloss, ließ hier eine grundlegende Kunstsammlung mit Werken aus Spanien und Portugal entstehen, erläutert Kengo Kuma. Das 12 679 m² große Grundstück weist als Besonderheit einen Kanal auf. Dazu Kuma: „Um Kanal und Museum zu einer Einheit zu verbinden, habe ich einen Zwischenraum entlang des Kanals geschaffen und eine Promenade für die Bewohner der Stadt angelegt. Dies ist ein Ort zur Würdigung von Kunstwerken. Steinlamellen schützen vor der starken Sonneneinstrahlung und sorgen für eine luftige, angenehme Verschattung." Eine wie eine „Glasbox" gestaltete Brücke führt über den Kanal her und ist für die Besucher des Museums weithin sichtbar. Vom Dach des Gebäudes, das auch als Galerie benutzt wird, bietet sich ein Blick auf den Hafen von Nagasaki.

Mit einer Grundfläche von 6248 m² und einer Gesamtfläche von 9898 m² ist das Museum ein großes Gebäude, das mit der für den Architekten typischen Sensibilität und Intelligenz entwickelt wurde. Kengo Kuma äußert sich recht offen über bestimmte Aspekte des Entwurfs. So sagt er: „In Nagasaki habe ich ein neues Detail für die Auflage der Steinlamellen entwickelt, indem ich massive Stahlstützen benutzte. Nagasaki im Süden Japans ist bekannt für seine Verandenarchitektur im Kolonialstil mit Spalieren aus Holz. Das Detail, das ich hier verwendete, ist eine moderne Version dieser traditionellen Architektur. Es ist auch eine Kritik an der modernen japanischen Architektur, die sowohl das Klima vor Ort als auch die Landschaft ignoriert."

Comme l'explique Kengo Kuma, le fait que Nagasaki ait été le seul port ouvert lorsque le Japon était isolé du reste du monde explique qu'il possède une substantielle collection d'art espagnol et portugais. L'une des caractéristiques du terrain de 12 679 m² était la présence d'un canal. « Pour que le canal ne fasse qu'un avec le musée, j'ai créé un volume intermédiaire le long de celui-ci. J'en ai fait une promenade pour les citadins qui est, en même temps, un nouveau lieu pour la découverte d'œuvres d'art. Cet espace est protégé du soleil par des brise-soleil de pierre qui créent une ombre agréable et aérée. » Une passerelle de verre « en forme de boîte » traverse le canal, désormais visible par tous les visiteurs du musée. Le toit sert également d'espace d'exposition et offre une vue sur le port. » Avec une emprise au sol de 6248 m² et une surface utile de 9898 m², il s'agit d'un grand bâtiment traité avec la subtilité et l'intelligence dont l'architecte a toujours fait preuve. Kengo Kuma s'exprime très volontiers sur certains aspects de son projet : « À Nagasaki, j'ai mis au point de nouveaux supports pour les brise-soleil de pierre, à base de colonnes en acier massif. Nagasaki, dans le Japon du Sud, est connue pour son architecture à vérandas de style colonial et leurs claustras en lattis de bois. Le système que j'utilise est une version contemporaine de cette architecture traditionnelle, c'est aussi une critique d'une architecture japonaise contemporaine qui ignore à la fois le climat et le paysage. »

Straddling a canal, the Museum is essentially divided into two parts, linked by a bridge. The architect has given a more open aspect to the structure nearer to the water.

Der Museumsbau besteht aus zwei Teilen entlang eines Kanals, die durch eine Brücke miteinander verbunden sind. Der Architekt hat den näher am Wasser stehenden Gebäudeteil offener gestaltet als dessen Gegenstück.

Enjambant sur un canal, le musée est divisé en deux parties reliées par une passerelle. L'architecte a donné un aspect plus ouvert au bâtiment en bordure de l'eau.

1.gate plaza
2.canal-side plaza
3.canal-side corridor
4.entrance
5.reference , museum shop
6.public gallery
7.loading dock 1
8.canal-side lobby
9.storage
10.storage anteroom
11.temporary storage
12.conservation room
13.photo studio
14.loading dock 2
15.office
16.director's office
17.meeting room
18.study room
19.machine room
20.pool
21.pedestrian bridge
22.pedestrian
23.private parking

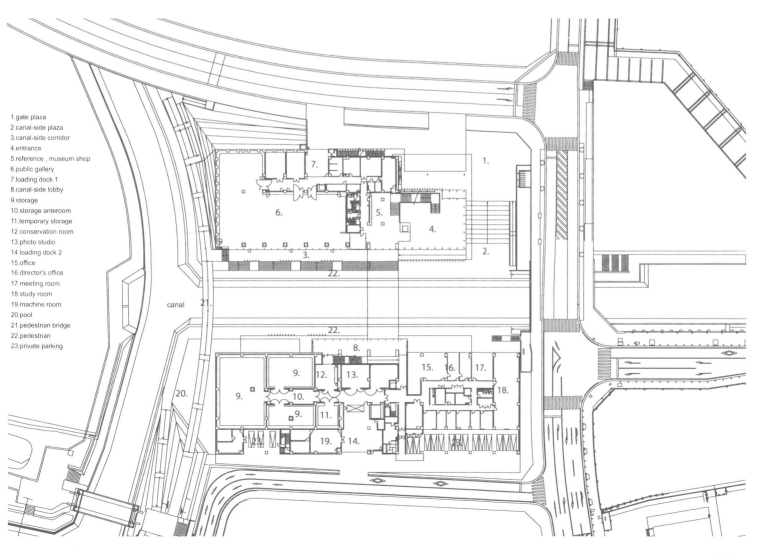

Kengo Kuma's use of light, vertical elements reduces the apparent bulk of the edifice, making it look lighter than it actually is. The differing treatment of the two main sections of the museum also enlivens its appearance.

Mit leichten, vertikalen Elementen hat Kengo Kuma die Masse des Gebäudes optisch reduziert, so dass es weniger massiv wirkt, als es tatsächlich ist. Auch die unterschiedliche Gestaltung der beiden Hauptgebäudeteile belebt das Erscheinungsbild.

La mise en œuvre de la lumière par des éléments verticaux diminue la masse apparente de l'édifice qui paraît plus léger qu'il n'est en réalité. La différence de traitement des deux principales parties du musée anime également l'aspect de l'ensemble.

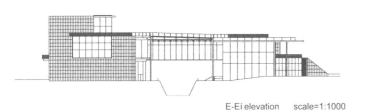

E-Ei elevation   scale=1:1000

D-Di elevation   scale=1:1000

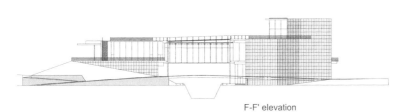

F-F' elevation

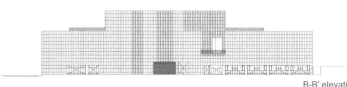

B-B' elevatio

A-A' elevation

C-C' elevatio

12

FUMIHIKO MAKI

MAKI AND ASSOCIATES
Hillside West Building C
13-4 Hachiyama-cho
Shibuya-ku
Tokyo 150-0035

Tel: + 81 3 37 80 38 80
Fax: + 81 3 37 80 38 81

e-mail: www.inquiry@maki-
and-associates.co.jp
Web: www.maki-and-
associates.co.jp

Born in Tokyo in 1928, **FUMIHIKO MAKI** received his Bachelor of Architecture degree from the University of Tokyo in 1952, and Master of Architecture degrees from the Cranbrook Academy of Art (1953) and the Harvard Graduate School of Design (1954). He worked for Skidmore, Owings & Merrill in New York (1954–55) and Sert Jackson and Associates in Cambridge, Massachusetts (1955–58) before creating his own firm, Maki and Associates, in Tokyo in 1965. Notable buildings include: the Fujisawa Municipal Gymnasium, Fujisawa, Kanagawa (1984); Spiral, Minato-ku, Tokyo (1985); the National Museum of Modern Art, Sakyo-ku, Kyoto (1986); the Tepia, Minato-ku, Tokyo (1989); the Nippon Convention Center Makuhari Messe, Chiba, Chiba (1989); Tokyo Metropolitan Gymnasium, Shibuya, Tokyo (1990); and the Center for the Arts Yerba Buena Gardens, San Francisco, California (1993). Recent projects have included: the Nippon Convention Center Makuhari Messe Phase II, Chiba, Chiba (completed in 1997), and the Hillside West buildings (completed in 1998), part of his ongoing Hillside Terrace project. More recent and current work includes the Yokohama Bayside Tower, Yokohama, Kanagawa (2003); the TV Asahi Broadcast Center, Minato-ku, Tokyo (2003); the Niigata International Convention Center, Niigata (2003); the MIT Media Laboratory Expansion, Cambridge, Massachusetts (2004); the National Language Research Institute, Tachikawa, Tokyo (2004); the Washington University Visual Arts and Design Center, St Louis, Missouri (2004); and the Nakatsu City Museum, Nakatsu, Oita (2005). Fumihiko Maki is also working on a tower for the United Nations in New York, a new museum of Islamic Art for the Aga Khan (Toronto) as well as a building for the Aga Khan's Ismaili community in Ottawa.

TV ASAHI HEADQUARTERS TOKYO 2001-03

FLOOR AREA: 73 700 m²
CLIENT: TV Asahi Corporation
COST: $350 million

The Roppongi Hills project, which includes a very large tower by KPF, is in fact an 11-hectare development area that includes apartment buildings, a cinema complex, a hotel and shopping arcades as well as offices. TV Asahi, one of Japan's five major private broadcasting companies, was a landowner in the area and has worked for the past 17 years to bring about the construction of its headquarters on a 16 368 m² site at the southeastern corner of Roppongi Hills. Fumihiko Maki, as might be expected, designed a much more subtle and attractive building, although, with its eight stories and three basements for a total floor area of 73 700 m², the steel and reinforced-concrete building is not small. Despite this considerable size, Fumihiko Maki has succeeded in maintaining the kind of attention to quality and space that is typical of his work. The architect explains that "The shape of the building responds to the curves of the two adjacent major streets and the natural contours of the site, creating a round shaped space that envelops visitors with a feeling of warmth. The bird's-eye view of the building resembles a Buddhist wooden drum or a fish head." One attractive feature of the building that is immediately visible to visitors is the series of works of art commissioned, in good part at the architect's suggestion. Included are the works "Guardian Stone" by Martin Puryear; "Counter Void" by Tatsuo Miyajima, and "Wall Drawing # 948" by Sol LeWitt, a brightly colored painting with circular bands of color that graces the entrance to the office area on the ground floor.

Das Bauvorhaben auf den Hügeln von Roppongi, zu dem ein gewaltiges Hochhaus von KPF gehört, ist ein 11 ha großes Stadtentwicklungsgebiet mit Wohnbauten, Kinokomplex und Hotel, Einkaufspassagen und Bürohäusern. TV Asahi, einer von Japans fünf größten Fernsehsendern, besaß ein großes Grundstück in diesem Viertel und hatte sich 17 Jahre lang um den Bau seiner Sendezentrale auf einem 16 368 m² großen Gelände im südöstlichen Abschnitt der Roppongi-Hügel bemüht. Wie zu erwarten war, entwarf Maki ein viel raffinierteres and attraktiveres Gebäude als sonst üblich, obwohl der Bau aus Stahl und Stahlbeton mit seinen acht Ober- und drei Untergeschossen und einer Gesamtgeschossfläche von 73 700 m² nicht gerade klein ist. Trotz des umfangreichen Raumprogramms gelang es Maki auch hier das für sein Werk typische Raumgefühl und Qualitätsbewusstsein

zu entfalten. Er erklärte dazu: „Die Form des Gebäudes folgt den zwei geschwungenen angrenzenden Hauptverkehrsstraßen und der natürlichen Beschaffenheit des Baugeländes. Daraus ergab sich ein runder Bau, der Besuchern ein Gefühl der Wärme vermittelt. Aus der Vogelperspektive ähnelt er einer buddhistischen Holztrommel oder einem Fischkopf." Besondere Attraktionen, die Besuchern sofort auffallen, sind die Kunstwerke, die zu einem Gutteil auf Anregung des Architekten in Auftrag gegeben wurden, darunter „Guardian Stone" von Martin Puryear, „Counter Void" von Tatsuo Miyajima und „Wall Drawing # 948" von Sol LeWitt, ein farbenfrohes Gemälde mit Farbringen, das die ebenerdige Eingangshalle des Bürobereichs schmückt.

Le projet des collines de Roppongi est une opération de promotion immobilière de 11 hectares qui comprend une énorme tour de bureaux signée KPF, des immeubles d'appartements, un complexe de cinémas, un hôtel, des galeries marchandes. TV Asahi, l'une cinq grandes sociétés privées de télévision japonaises était propriétaire d'un terrain de 16 368 m² à l'angle sud-est des collines de Roppongi et cherchait depuis 17 ans à y construire son siège. Fumihiko Maki, comme on pouvait s'y attendre, a conçu un immeuble subtil et séduisant en béton armé et acier qui, avec ses 73 700 m², ses huit niveaux de haut et trois en sous-sol, n'est en rien petit. Malgré ces dimensions considérables, l'architecte a réussi à maintenir le niveau d'attention au traitement des espaces et à la qualité de réalisation qui sont caractéristiques de son œuvre. Il explique que « la forme de l'immeuble correspond à celle des deux grands axes de circulation qui le longent et aux contours naturels du terrain. Cette forme arrondie enveloppe le visiteur d'un sentiment chaleureux. Vu du ciel, l'immeuble fait penser à un tambour bouddhique en bois ou à une tête de poisson ». Une des caractéristiques intéressantes de ce projet, visible de tous les visiteurs, est un ensemble d'œuvres d'art commandées en grande partie sur les conseils de l'architecte. On y trouve « Guardian Stone » de Martin Puryer, « Counter Void » de Tatsuo Miyajima et « Wall Drawing # 948 » de Sol Lewitt, peinture de couleurs vives à motifs circulaires qui anime l'entrée de la zone des bureaux au rez-de-chaussée.

Located near the heart of the bustling Roppongi district of Tokyo, Maki's TV Asahi building combines a high density with large, open spaces, where works of art take their place in a natural way.

Das TV Asahi-Gebäude von Fumihiko Maki liegt unweit des Zentrums des belebten Roppongi-Bezirks von Tokio. Trotz der hohen Bebauungsdichte bietet es große, offene Räume, in denen die Kunstwerke den ihnen angemessenen Platz gefunden haben.

Situé non loin du cœur du quartier très animé de Roppongi à Tokyo, l'immeuble de TV Asahi conçu par Maki associe une forte densité à de vastes espaces ouverts où des œuvres d'art trouvent leur place de manière naturelle.

Seen at night, the large building glows from within, as transparent as it seems to be opaque during the day. Very generous ceiling heights in the entrance areas contribute to the overall effect of lightness in the image seen above.

Bei Nacht leuchtet der große Bau von innen heraus und gibt sich völlig transparent, während er tagsüber geschlossen wirkt. Hohe Decken im Eingangsbereich tragen zum Gesamteindruck von Licht und Leichtigkeit bei (oben).

La nuit, ce vaste immeuble scintille, aussi transparent qu'il peut sembler opaque pendant le jour. Les très généreuses hauteurs de plafond des zones d'entrée contribuent à une impression générale de légèreté, comme le montre l'image ci-dessus.

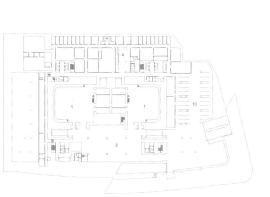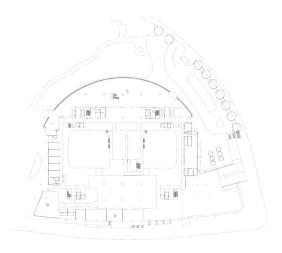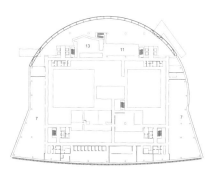

Fumihiko Maki was personally involved in the choice of the artists who worked on the building, such as Martin Puryear, Sol LeWitt, or Tatsuo Miyajima ("Counter Void", above). To the left, the entrance lobby of the building.

Fumihiko Maki war persönlich an der Auswahl der Künstler beteiligt, die zur Ausstattung des Gebäudes beitrugen, darunter Martin Puryear, Sol LeWitt und Tatsuo Miyajima („Counter Void", oben). Links eine Innenansicht des Eingangsfoyers.

Fumihiko Maki s'est personnellement impliqué dans le choix des artistes invités à intervenir sur l'immeuble, comme Martin Puryear, Sol LeWitt ou Tatsuo Miyajima dont on voit l'œuvre « Counter Void » ci-dessus. À gauche, le hall d'entrée de l'immeuble.

13

KAZUYO SEJIMA + RYUE NISHIZAWA / SANAA

**KAZUYO SEJIMA + RYUE
NISHIZAWA / SANAA**
7-A Shinagawa-Soko
2-2-35 Higashi-Shinagawa
Shinagawa-ku
Tokyo 140

Tel: +81 3 34 50 17 54
Fax: +81 3 34 50 17 57
e-mail: sanaa@sanaa.co.jp
Web: www.sanaa.co.jp

Born in Ibaraki Prefecture in 1956, **KAZUYO SEJIMA** received her Master's degree in architecture from Japan Women's University in 1981, and went to work in the office of Toyo Ito the same year. She established Kazuyo Sejima and Associates in Tokyo in 1987. She has been a visiting lecturer at Japan Women's University and at Waseda University since 1994. **RYUE NISHIZAWA** was born in Tokyo in 1966, and graduated from the National University in Yokohama in 1990. He began working with Sejima the same year, and the pair created the new firm Kazuyo Sejima + Ryue Nishizawa / SANAA in 1995. He has been a Visiting Professor at the Harvard School of Design and at the National University in Yokohama. The built work of Kazuyo Sejima includes: the Saishunkan Seiyaku Women's Dormitory in Kumamoto, Kumamoto (1990–91); Pachinko Parlor I, Hitachi, Ibaraki (1992–93); Pachinko Parlor II, Nakamachi, Ibaraki (1993); Villa in the Forest, Tateshina, Nagano (1993–94); Chofu Station Police Box, Tokyo (1993–94); Pachinko Parlor III, Hitachi Ibaraki (1995). The work of SANAA presently includes the Glass Pavilion of the Toledo Museum of Art, a theater and cultural center in Almere, an extension of the Instituto Valenciano de Arte Moderno (IVAM), Valencia, Spain, and the building for the New Museum of Contemporary Art in New York. Kazuyo Sejima and Ryue Nishizawa recently won the competitions to design the Learning Center of the EPFL in Lausanne, Switzerland, and for the new building of the Louvre Museum in Lens, North of France.

21ST CENTURY MUSEUM OF CONTEMPORARY ART
KANAZAWA
2002 · 04

FLOOR AREA: 27 920 m² (including parking lot)
CLIENT: City of Kanazawa
COST: $97 million

When Kanazawa, a city of 456 000 people located on the Sea of Japan, is mentioned, most people who know the country immediately think of its temples and gardens, in particular Korakuen, considered one of the three great gardens of Japan. And yet, since its opening on October 9, 2004, the 21st Century Museum of Contemporary Art has attracted many interested in recent architecture to a site located diagonally opposite the entrance to Korakuen. Laid out in very simple terms, as a 112.5-meter-diameter circle, the museum is larger than most works by SANAA, and yet it retains much of the magical ambiguity seen in earlier work. Exhibition areas are in good part designed in the "white cube" mode, though their ceiling heights vary from four to twelve meters. The fully glazed curved façade of the building has no apparent front entrance and, indeed, it is possible simply to enter the facility and walk around its outer periphery, seeing some art, without ever paying an entry fee. The undulating garden, with trees replanted from the school that had existed on the site, participates in rendering the architecture more convivial, since views toward the outside are frequently offered from within the museum. An inner courtyard with a vegetal work by Patrick Berger, and a number of other "surprises" await visitors, demonstrating that an unexpected form of modernity can emerge from the most basic geometric forms. With a respectable collection of Japanese and Western artworks, the 21st Century Museum of Contemporary Art has put the city on the map of contemporary creativity.

Wenn man Kanazawa erwähnt, eine Stadt mit 456 000 Einwohnern am Japanischen Meer, denken Landeskundige sofort an seine Tempel und Gärten, vor allem an Korakuen, einen der drei schönsten und berühmtesten Gärten Japans. Seit seiner Eröffnung am 9. Oktober 2004 hat das Museum für Gegenwartskunst des 21. Jahrhunderts viele an neuester Architektur Interessierte an einen Ortgelockt, der schräg gegenüber vom Eingang zum Korakuen-Garten liegt. Das Museum mit seinem einfachen Grundriss in Kreisform mit einem Durchmesser 112,5 m ist größer als die meisten Bauten von SANAA und weist doch viel von der magischen Ambiguität ihrer früheren Projekte auf. Die Ausstellungsräume sind zu einem Gutteil nach Art „weißer Würfel" gestaltet, deren Deckenhöhen zwischen vier und zwölf Metern variieren. Die voll verglaste, geschwungene Fassade weist keinen eindeutig als solchen erkennbaren Haupteingang auf. Tatsächlich kann man das Gebäude betreten und den Rundgangkorridor hinter der Fassade durchlaufen – wobei man einige Kunstwerke zu sehen bekommt –, ohne Eintritt zu zahlen. Der mehrfach geschwungene Garten mit alten, umgesetzten Bäumen vom Gelände der Schule, die früher hier stand, trägt zur angenehmen Atmosphäre des Museums bei, da es durch zahlreiche Öffnungen Durch- und Ausblicke in den Garten bietet. Ein Innenhof mit einer Pflanzenwand von Patrick Berger und eine Reihe weiterer „Überraschungen" erwarten die Besucher. Dieser Museumsbau zeigt, dass elementarste geometrische Formen eine ungewöhnliche Modernität erzeugen können. Mit seiner beachtlichen Sammlung japanischer, europäischer und amerikanischer Kunst hat das Museum für Gegenwartskunst des 21. Jahrhunderts die Stadt Kanazawa auf die Weltkarte des zeitgemäßen künstlerischen Schaffens gesetzt.

Le nom de Kanazawa, ville de 456 000 habitants au bord de la mer du Japon, évoque surtout des temples et des jardins, en particulier celui de Korakuen considéré comme l'un de trois premiers jardins du pays. Aujourd'hui cependant, beaucoup d'amateurs d'architecture et d'art contemporain découvrent ce nouveau musée d'art contemporain inauguré le 9 octobre 2004 juste en face de l'entrée du Korakuen. De plan très simple – un cercle de 112,5 m de diamètre – il est plus vaste que la plupart des réalisations de l'agence SANAA à ce jour et a néanmoins conservé beaucoup de l'ambiguïté magique si appréciée dans ses précédents travaux. Les salles d'exposition sont en grande partie conçues dans un esprit formel de « cube blanc », même si leur hauteur varie de 4 à 12 m. La façade circulaire entièrement vitrée ne possède apparemment aucune entrée et il est même possible d'en faire le tour et de voir quelques œuvres d'art exposées sans payer de ticket d'entrée. Le jardin en courbes, dont les arbres sont ceux d'une école qui existait antérieurement sur le site, contribue à rendre cette architecture plus conviviale puisque le musée s'ouvre fréquemment vers sur son environnement. Une cour intérieure dont l'aménagement végétal est dû à Patrick Berger et un certain nombre d'autres « surprises » attendent le visiteur, illustration qu'une forme inattendue de modernité peut toujours jaillir même des formes les plus géométriques. Avec sa très respectable collection d'œuvres japonaises et occidentales, le Musée d'art contemporain du XXIe siècle a remis Kanazawa sur la carte de la créativité d'aujourd'hui.

Administrative Office
Curatorial Office
Theater 21
Long-Term Project
Info Terminal
Meeting Room
Foyer
EV
Gallery 11
Rest Corner
Courtyard
Gallery 8
Museum Shop
Design Gallery
Foyer
People's Gallery
Rest Corner
Gallery 12
Gallery 10
Gallery 9
Gallery 7
Restaurant
Courtyard
Gallery 14
Courtyard
Foyer
Foyer
EV
EV
Gallery 1
Turrell Room
Gallery 13
Gallery 5
Gallery 6
Kapoor Room
Lecture Hall
Courtyard
Rest Corner
Gallery 4
Rest Corner
Gallery 3
Gallery 2
Rest Corner
Library
Lounge
Kid's Studio

Although the round plan of the museum might not seem to be ideal at first glance, the architects have inscribed a series of square, rectangular or round galleries within its circumference that give an impression of great variety to visitors. At night, the museum glows from within.

Die runde Bauform mag auf den ersten Blick für ein Museum nicht ideal erscheinen, die Architekten haben sie aber in eine Reihe quadratischer, rechteckiger und runder Ausstellungsräume unterteilt, die Besuchern den Eindruck großer Vielfältigkeit vermitteln. Nachts leuchtet das Museum von innen heraus.

Bien que l'idée d'un plan circulaire pour un musée ne semble pas idéale au premier abord, les architectes ont réussi à y inscrire une série de salles carrées, rectangulaires et rondes, ce qui donne une grande impression de variété. La nuit, le musée irradie de son éclairage intérieur.

Courtyards within the museum allow light into the galleries and give space to such unusual works as Patrick Blanc's vegetal wall "Green Bridge", 2004 (both images below).

Die Innenhöfe bringen Tageslicht in die Galerien und geben so ungewöhnlichen Werken wie Patrick Blancs Pflanzenwand „Green Bridge" aus dem Jahr 2004 (unten) Raum.

Ci-dessous : les cours intérieures du musée amènent la lumière jusque dans les galeries ou se transforment en espaces d'exposition pour des œuvres curieuses comme le mur végétal de Patrick Blanc « Green Bridge » (2004).

Floor-to-ceiling glazing in many locations allows the otherwise white and rather antiseptic spaces to take on the colors of the sky. A square glass gallery in a courtyard permits works featuring plants to be shown, for example, although its walls can be rendered opaque.

Raumhohe Verglasungen lassen an vielen Stellen die ansonsten eher steril wirkenden weißen Räume die Farben des Himmels annehmen. Ein würfelförmiger Glaspavillon in einem Hof ermöglicht die Ausstellung von Kunstwerken mit Pflanzen; seine Wände können auch undurchsichtig gemacht werden.

À de nombreux endroits, des vitrages sol-plafond permettent aux volumes blancs et assez aseptisés de se teinter des couleurs du ciel. Dans une cour, une galerie en forme de cube de verre permet d'exposer des œuvres à base de plantes, mais ses murs peuvent être opacifiés.

CHRISTIAN DIOR OMOTESANDO TOKYO 2001·04

FLOOR AREA: 1492 m²
CLIENT: Christian Dior
COST: not disclosed

Located quite close to Toyo Ito's Tod's building and not far from Tadao Ando's hhstyle.com/casa, both featured in this book, SANAA's structure for Dior is in the heart of the Omotesando-Harajuku district, where Tokyo has shown that it has as much if not more style than any Western city. The building is "wrapped" in an unusual way, with an outside layer of clear glass, lined with translucent acrylic. At 30 meters tall, and set into a trapezoidal site on Omotesando Avenue, the Dior building has one basement level and the first three floors devoted to retail sales. An event space on the fourth floor and a rooftop garden complete the design. The actual number of floors is not readily apparent from the exterior, emphasizing the impression of ambiguity generated by the building. Interior work was done, amongst others by Dior Homme designer Hedi Slimane for the basement level. The thermo-formed acrylic drapes visible from the inside of the building in any case give it a degree of internal congruity with the façade designs. With this building, Sejima shows that a deliberately changeable or ambiguous appearance can indeed be coherent with the work of one of the most colorful and dynamic fashion designers of the moment—John Galliano. Indeed, in spite of Galliano's flamboyance, the store sells something of the classic permanence attached to the name of its founder Christian Dior, and SANAA's shimmering glass object actually seems entirely appropriate to that image of beauty.

SANAAs Dior-Gebäude liegt nicht weit von Toyo Itos Gebäude für Tod's und Tado Andos „hhstyle.com/casa", die beide in diesem Buch vorgestellt werden, und mitten im Bezirk Omotesando-Harajuku, in dem die Metropole Tokio bewiesen hat, dass sie mindestens so viel Stil hat wie jede Großstadt der westlichen Welt. Das Gebäude hat eine ungewöhnliche „Hülle" – eine äußere aus Glas und eine innere aus transluzentem Acryl. Es ist 30 m hoch und steht auf einem trapezförmigen Grundstück an der Omotesando Avenue. Das Untergeschoss, das Erdgeschoss und zwei Obergeschosse des Dior-Gebäudes werden von Verkaufsflächen eingenommen. Ein Veranstaltungsbereich und ein Dachgarten vervollständigen es. Die Anzahl der Geschossebenen ist von außen nur schwer zu erkennen. Diese Ambi-

guität ist beabsichtigt. Die Innenarchitektur stammt unter anderem vom Dior-Homme-Designer Hedi Slimane, der das Untergeschoss gestaltete. Die thermoplastisch geformte innere Acrylhülle passt zur Ästhetik der Fassade. Mit diesem Entwurf demonstrierte Sejima, dass ein bewusst veränderlich und uneindeutig gestaltetes Gebäude mit dem Werk eines der schillerndsten und dynamischsten Modedesigner unserer Zeit – nämlich John Galliano – harmonieren kann. Tatsächlich hat dieser Bau Gallianos Extravaganz zum Trotz etwas von der klassischen Zeitlosigkeit des Firmengründers Christian Dior. SANAAs schimmerndes Glasobjekt scheint für dieses Schönheitsideal „maßgeschneidert" zu sein.

Très proche de l'immeuble Tod's de Toyo Ito et non loin de la hhstyle.com/casa de Ando, tous deux présentés dans cet ouvrage, le projet de SANAA pour Dior se trouve au cœur du quartier d'Omotesando-Harajuku, où Tokyo affiche un style qui n'a rien à envier aux grandes capitales occidentales. L'immeuble est enveloppé de façon surprenante d'une peau extérieure en verre transparent doublé d'acrylique translucide. Haut de 30 m et construit sur un terrain de forme trapézoïdale, ses trois premiers niveaux au-dessus d'un sous-sol sont consacrés à la vente au public. Un espace pour réceptions au quatrième niveau et un jardin sur le toit complètent le projet. Le nombre d'étages est difficile à déchiffrer de l'extérieur, ce qui renforce l'impression générale d'ambiguïté. L'aménagement intérieur a été réalisé, entre autres, par le styliste homme de Dior, Hedi Slimane, pour le sous-sol. Les drapés en acrylique thermoformé visibles de l'intérieur font lien avec la façade. Avec cette réalisation, Sejima montre qu'une apparence délibérément changeante ou ambiguë peut venir en cohérence avec l'œuvre d'un des créateurs de mode les plus effervescents du moment, John Galliano. Cependant, en dehors de la flamboyance des modèles exposés, le magasin transmet quelque chose de la permanence classique attachée au nom du fondateur, Christian Dior, et ce bel objet de verre frissonnant imaginé par SANAA semble parfaitement approprié à son image de la beauté.

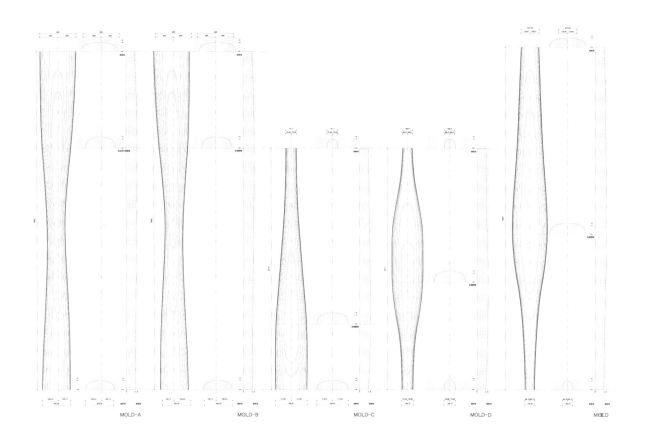

MOLD-A   MOLD-B   MOLD-C   MOLD-D   MOLD-E

The translucent acrylic used by the architects inside the glass façade gives a milky ambiguity to the entire 30-meter-high building located not far from the Tod's Building by Toyo Ito. With its supporting structure invisible from the exterior, the architecture seems to float above Omotesando Avenue.

Die von den Architekten hinter der Glasfassade eingesetzten transluzenten Acrylplatten verleihen dem nicht weit von Toyo Itos Tod's Gebäude gelegenen, 30 m hohen Bau milchige Unbestimmtheit. Da sein Tragwerk von außen nicht zu sehen ist, scheint es über der Omotesando Avenue zu schweben.

L'acrylique transparent utilisé par les architectes en arrière de la façade de verre crée une ambiguïté laiteuse sur toute la hauteur de cet immeuble de 30 m de haut, non loin de celui de Tod's conçu par Toyo Ito. Sa structure restant invisible de l'extérieur, l'architecture semble flotter au-dessus de l'avenue Omotesando.

14

YOSHIO TANIGUCHI

YOSHIO TANIGUCHI & ASSOCIATES
Edomizaka Mori Building 8F
4-1-40, Toranomon
Minato-ku
Tokyo 105-0001

Tel: + 81 3 34 38 12 47
Fax: + 81 3 34 38 12 48

YOSHIO TANIGUCHI was born in Tokyo in 1937. He received a Bachelor's degree in Mechanical Engineering from Keio University in 1960, and a Master's of Architecture degree from the Harvard Graduate School of Design in 1964. He worked in the office of Kenzo Tange from 1964 to 1972. He created Taniguchi, Takamiya and Associates in 1975, and Yoshio Taniguchi and Associates in 1979. His built work includes: the Tokyo Sea Life Park, Tokyo (1989); the Marugame Genichiro-Inokuma Museum of Contemporary Art and Marugame City Library, Marugame (1991); the Toyota Municipal Museum of Art, Toyota City (1995); the Tokyo Kasai Rinkai Park View Point Visitors Center, Tokyo (1995); the Tokyo National Museum Gallery of Horyuji Treasures, Tokyo (1997–99), featured here; and the complete renovation and expansion of the Museum of Modern Art in New York. He won the project in a 1997 invited competition against Wiel Arets, Steven Holl, Rem Koolhaas, Herzog & de Meuron, Toyo Ito, Dominique Perrault, Bernard Tschumi, Rafael Viñoly, and Williams & Tsien. Inaugurated on November 20, 2004, the new MoMA met with some criticism, but it gave Taniguchi an international visibility that he had never had before. He is completing the Kyoto National Museum, Centennial Hall (2006), and beginning work on the Asia House in Houston.

GALLERY OF HORYUJI TREASURES
TOKYO 1997-99

FLOOR AREA: 4030 m²
CLIENT: Ministry of Education
and Ministry of Construction
COST: not disclosed

Set in the grounds of the Tokyo National Museum in Ueno Park in Tokyo, this structure by Yoshio Taniguchi was designed to house a number of works originally from the Horyuji Temple in Nara. The collection was donated to the Imperial Household by the temple in 1878, and approximately 300 cultural properties became national property after World War II. The building that originally stood on the same site served essentially to preserve the works. The new building, designed for the Ministry of Education and Ministry of Construction, covers an area of 1934 m² and has a total floor area of 4030 m². It is a four-story structure built of reinforced concrete with a steel frame. Inspired by the wooden boxes used to protect precious art objects in Japan, the design includes a high metal canopy, a glazed entrance area that is separated by a concrete wall from the almost completely darkened inner exhibition area. Open on two sides to the garden environment with a shallow basin marking the entrance area, this building has a jewel-like precision in its construction. As Yoshio Taniguchi has said, "Out of a desire to respect both the sublime works to be displayed and the natural setting, I made it my goal in designing the new Gallery of Horyuji Treasures to create on the site an environment of a kind that has become all too rare in present-day Tokyo, that is, an environment characterized by tranquility, order and dignity."

Dieser Bau von Yoshio Taniguchi auf dem Gelände des Nationalmuseums im Ueno Park von Tokio sollte Kunstwerke aus dem Horyuji-Tempel in Nara aufnehmen. 1878 hatte der Tempel diese Sammlung von rund 300 Objekten dem Kaiser geschenkt; nach dem Zweiten Weltkrieg ging diese in staatlichen Besitz über. Das alte Gebäude an derselben Stelle hatte hauptsächlich als Magazin gedient. Der vom Erziehungsministerium und vom Bauministerium in Auftrag gegebene viergeschossige Neubau aus Stahlbeton mit Stahlrahmentragwerk hat eine Grundfläche von 1934 m² und eine Gesamtgeschossfläche von 4030 m². Inspiration für die Gestaltung lieferten die in Japan üblichen Holzkästen zur Aufbewahrung kostbarer Objekte. Der Innenraum wird von einem hohen Dach überspannt; die Eingangshalle ist nach vorne voll verglast. Eine Betonwand trennt sie von den weitgehend abgedunkelten Ausstellungsräumen. Der Bau öffnet sich nach zwei Seiten zum Park (wobei der Eingangsbereich von einem seichten Wasserbecken markiert wird) und ist wie ein Brilliant von geschliffener Präzision. Taniguchi erklärt dazu: „Aus dem Wunsch heraus, sowohl die kostbaren Exponate als auch die natürliche Umgebung zu würdigen, nahm ich mir vor, aus der Galerie für die Kunstschätze von Horyuji einen Ort zu machen, der im heutigen Tokio allzu selten geworden ist – einen Ort der Ruhe, Ordnung und Würde."

Implanté au milieu des jardins du Musée national de Tokyo dans le parc d'Ueno à Tokyo, cette construction abrite un certain nombre d'œuvres qui appartenaient à l'origine au temple Horyuji de Nara. Cette collection a été offerte par le temple à la maison impériale en 1878 et 300 objets sont devenus propriété nationale après la Seconde Guerre mondiale. Le bâtiment antérieur qui existait au même endroit servait essentiellement à leur conservation. Le nouveau, conçu pour le ministère de l'Éducation et celui de la Construction, occupe une surface au sol de 1934 m² pour 4030 m² de surface utile. En béton armé sur ossature en acier, il comporte quatre niveaux. Inspiré des boîtes en bois qui servent à protéger les objets d'art précieux au Japon, il se caractérise par un vaste auvent métallique et une zone d'entrée entièrement vitrée, séparée par un mur de béton du volume d'exposition presque entièrement sombre. Ouvert des deux côtés sur le jardin et son entrée signalée par un bassin, ce petit musée a été réalisé avec une précision de joaillier. Comme Yoshio Taniguchi le précise : « Partant de mon désir de respecter à la fois ces œuvres sublimes et le cadre naturel, j'ai voulu concevoir... sur ce site un environnement d'un type devenu trop rare dans le Tokyo actuel, c'est-à-dire un environnement caractérisé par la sérénité, l'ordre et la dignité. »

Located in Ueno Park, the gallery is approached along the walkway seen in the image above. Visitors then turn right and walk next to a shallow pond before crossing over into the building.

Zur Galerie im Ueno-Park führt ein langer Fußweg (oben). Besucher wenden sich dann nach rechts, gehen an einem seichten Wasserbecken entlang und überqueren es, um zum Eingang zu gelangen.

Située dans le parc d'Ueno, la galerie se trouve à l'extrémité d'une l'allée (ci-dessus). Les visiteurs tournent ensuite vers la droite et longent un bassin en creux avant de le traverser pour pénétrer dans le bâtiment.

A good part of the building is given over to a brightly lit entrance area, while the actual works of art are presented in identical glass cases in a darkened space (below).

Ein Gutteil des Gebäudes wird von der lichtdurchfluteten Eingangshalle eingenommen, während die Kunstwerke in einem abgedunkelten Raum in identischen Vitrinen ausgestellt sind (unten).

Une bonne partie du bâtiment est consacrée à une zone d'entrée brillamment éclairée tandis que les œuvres d'art sont présentées à l'intérieur de vitrines de verre toutes identiques dans une salle à l'éclairage réduit (en bas).

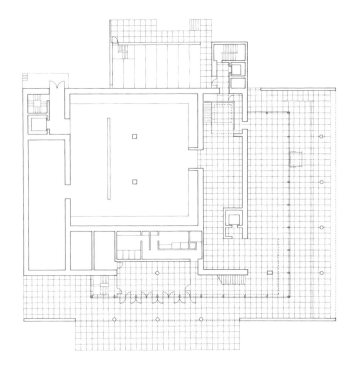

15

TEZUKA ARCHITECTS

TEZUKA ARCHITECTS
1-19-9-3F Todoroki
Setagaya
Tokyo 158-0082

Tel: + 81 3 37 03 70 56
Fax: + 81 3 37 03 70 38
e-mail: tez@sepia.ocn.ne.jp
Web: www.tezuka-arch.com

TAKAHARU TEZUKA, born in Tokyo in 1964, received his degrees from the Musashi Institute of Technology (1987), and from the University of Pennsylvania (1990). He worked with Richard Rogers Partnership Ltd. (1994), and established Tezuka Architects the same year. Born in Kanagawa in 1969, **YUI TEZUKA** was educated at the Musashi Institute of Technology, and the Bartlett School of Architecture, University College of London. The practice has completed about a dozen private houses, and won the competition for the Matsunoyama Museum of Natural Sciences in 2000. Since then it has been based in Tokyo. Their work includes: the Soejima Hospital; Jyubako House; Shoe Box House; Big Window House; Observatory House; Forest House; Clipping Corner House; Floating House; Engawa House; House to Catch the Sky III; Saw Roof House; Skylight House; Canopy House; Thin Wall House; Thin Roof House; Anthill House; Step House; House to Catch the Sky 2; House to Catch the Sky 1; Wall-less House; Roof House; Megaphone House; Machiya House; Light Gauge Steel House; and the Wood Deck House.

OBSERVATORY HOUSE
KAMAKURA 2004

AREA: 176 m²
CLIENT: not disclosed
COST: $720 000

The architects faced the challenge of offering a view toward the Pacific Ocean from this house, although the water is not visible from ground level. Working with a 137 m² site, they decided to use the maximum authorized height for a three-story structure ten meters high. An added reason for this configuration was that spectacular fireworks displays are organized from a beach on the opposite side of the bay. As Takaharu Tezuka says, "The final design looked like an observatory resting on the palm of a hand," thus explaining the name of the house. Covering just 55 m² on the ground, the residence has a total floor area of 176 m². As the architects explain their scheme, "The three sides of the house with a view over the ocean were built without walls. Instead, sliding glass panels were lined up with an equivalent number of shutters. The strong ocean wind makes it difficult to leave the windows open when it rains. But it is possible to pull the shutters and adjust the louvers, giving the house the looks of a kind of meteorological observation post. Luckily enough, the construction was completed in time for the fireworks display. Watching the colorful bursts above the crowd of spectators was an unforgettable finale."

Die Herausforderung des Bauauftrags bestand darin, dem Haus Ausblicke auf den Pazifik zu verschaffen, denn vom Bodenniveau aus sieht man ihn nicht. Die Architekten beschlossen daher, auf das 137 m² große Grundstück ein dreigeschossiges Haus mit der maximal zulässigen Bauhöhe von 10 m zu setzen. Ein weiterer Anreiz hierfür waren die spektakulären Feuerwerke, die auf einem Strand jenseits der Bucht veranstaltet werden. Takaharu Tezuka sagt: „Im endgültigen Entwurf sah das Haus wie eine Sternwarte auf einer Handfläche aus, was seinen Namen erklärt. Auf einer Grundfläche von nur 55 m² bietet es eine Wohnfläche von 176 m²." Laut Projekterläuterung der Architekten öffnet sich das Haus „auf drei Seiten mit großen Glasschiebetüren, die von ebenso vielen Holzläden verschlossen werden können, zum Pazifik. Die starken Winde vom Meer her machen es schwierig, die Fenster bei Regen offen zu lassen. Man kann aber die Holzläden schließen und die Lamellen so verstellen, dass das Haus wie eine Art Wetterstation aussieht. Zum Glück wurde das Haus noch vor dem großen Feuerwerk bezugsfertig. Die bunten Explosionen der Feuerwerkskörper hoch über den Köpfen der Zuschauer zu beobachten, war für uns ein unvergessliches Finale."

Les architectes étaient ici confrontés au problème d'offrir une vue sur le Pacifique, bien qu'il ne soit pas visible du rez-de-chaussée. Sur la base d'un terrain de 137 m², ils ont décidé de tirer profit de la hauteur maximum autorisée pour édifier une maison de 10 m de haut sur trois niveaux. Une des raisons supplémentaires de ce choix était la présence de spectacles de feux d'artifice spectaculaires organisés de l'autre côté de la baie. Comme l'explique Takaharu Tezuka : « Le projet final fait penser à un observatoire posé sur la paume de la main », ce qui explique le nom de la maison. Occupant tout juste 55 m² au sol, elle offre une surface utile de 176 m². « Les trois façades qui donnent sur l'océan n'ont pas de murs, remplacés par des panneaux de verre coulissants doublés de volets. La violence des vents marins ne permet guère de laisser les baies ouvertes par temps de pluie, mais il est possible de tirer les volets et de régler les persiennes, ce qui donne à la maison une allure son allure de poste d'observation météorologique. Heureusement, la maison a été achevée à temps pour les feux d'artifice. Regarder ces explosions de couleur par-dessus la foule des spectateurs a représenté un moment inoubliable. »

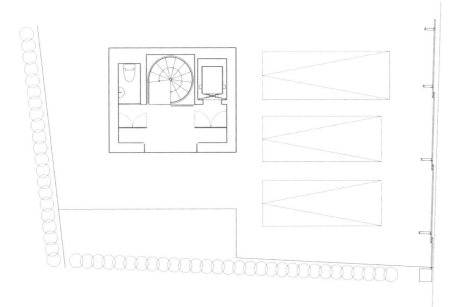

Extremely simple spaces with ample glazing offer open views toward the water. A spiral staircase rises toward the rooftop visible on the following double page.

Äußerst schlichte, großzügig verglaste Räume bieten freie Sicht zum Wasser hin. Eine Wendeltreppe führt zur Dachterrasse (nächste Doppelseite).

Les espaces extrêmement simples et généreusement vitrés donnent sur l'eau. Un escalier en spirale s'élève vers le toit en terrasse (double page suivante).

Even the bathtub is placed next to a fully glazed wall. The space above with its closed wooden shutters is the same as that visible on the facing page, seen from the opposite side.

Sogar die Badewanne steht vor einer Glaswand. Der Raum mit den geschlossenen hölzernen Fensterläden (oben) ist identisch mit dem Raum auf der gegenüber liegenden Seite – nur aus entgegengesetzter Perspektive.

Même la baignoire est disposée contre un mur entièrement en verre. L'espace audessus, à volets de bois fermés, est celui de la page ci-contre, vu de l'autre côté.

MATSUNOYAMA NATURAL SCIENCE MUSEUM

MATSUNOYAMA 2002-04

FLOOR AREA: 1248 m²
CLIENT: Matsunoyama-machi/
Secretariat of Tokamachi Regionwide
Municipal Corporation
COST: $6.5 million

Located approximately 200 km to the north of Tokyo in a region that has the heaviest snowfalls of Japan (up to five meters a year), the Matsunoyama Natural Science Museum was built without firm foundations because the building expands 20 cm in summer. A Corten steel tube designed to resist snow loads of up to 2000 tons meanders over a length of 111 meters, following the topography and allowing visitors to "experience the light and colors under the different depths of snow from 4 m deep to 30 m above the ground." Steel plates 6 mm thick weighing 500 tons were welded in place to the load-bearing steel structure, and four large windows made of 75 mm-thick Perspex and located at the turning points in the museum space permit direct observation with life under the snow. A 34-meter-high observation tower, the only element with a normal foundation, completes the project. Tezuka Architects describe the structure as a "submarine, with the tower its periscope," in a willful effort to contrast with the white natural winter landscape.

Das Naturwissenschaftliche Museum Matsunoyama liegt etwa 200 km nördlich von Tokio. In dieser Region gibt es die stärksten Schneefälle in Japan – der Schnee kann hier bis zu 5 m hoch liegen. Das Gebäude dehnt sich im Sommer 20 cm aus und hat daher keine festen Fundamente. Eine 111 m lange, mäandrierende Röhre aus Corten-Stahl, die Schneelasten bis 2000 t abfangen kann, folgt der Topografie und ermöglicht es dem Besucher, „das Licht und die Farben unter dem Schnee, der sich hier 4 bis 30 m hoch auftürmt, zu erleben". 6 mm dicke Stahlplatten mit einem Gesamtgewicht von 500 t wurden vor Ort an die tragende Stahl-konstruktion geschweißt. Vier große Fenster mit 75 mm dicken Perspex-Scheiben sind an den Eckpunkten des Museumsraums angeordnet. Von hier aus kann das Leben unter dem Schnee direkt beobachtet werden. Ein 34 m hoher Aussichtsturm, der einzige Teil des Museums mit herkömmlichen Fundamenten, komplettiert die Anlage. Tezuka Architects beschreiben das Gebäude als „ein U-Boot – mit dem Turm als Periskop". Der Turm stellt dabei einen gewollten Kontrast zur weißen Winterlandschaft her.

Situé à environ 200 km au nord de Tokyo dans une région qui connaît les plus importantes chutes de neige du Japon (jusqu'à 5 m), ce musée des Sciences naturelles a été construit sans fondations fixes car il se dilate de 20 cm en été. Il s'agit essentiellement d'un tube en acier Corten conçu pour résister à une charge de neige de 2000 tonnes, qui se fond dans la topographie sur une longueur de 111 m et permet aux visiteurs « de faire l'expérience de la lumière et des couleurs sous différentes épaisseurs de neige, de 4 m de profondeur jusqu'à 30 m au-dessus du niveau du sol ». Les 500 tonnes de tôles d'acier de 6 mm d'épaisseur ont été soudées sur place sur la structure porteuse en acier et quatre grandes baies fermées d'un panneau de Perspex de 75 mm d'épaisseur, positionnées aux angles de la structure pour faciliter l'observation directe de la vie sous la neige. Une tour d'observation de 34 m de haut, seul élément à posséder des fondations normales, complète l'ensemble. Tezuka Architects décrit ce musée comme « un sous-marin, dont la tour serait le périscope », volontairement conçu pour contraster avec le paysage hivernal enneigé.

The unusual, snake-like form of the museum permits visitors to take a tour under the deep winter snowfalls. The tower of the museum intentionally accentuates the building's similarity to a submerged submarine.

Die ungewöhnliche, schlangenähnliche Form des Museums ermöglicht Besuchern im Winter den Rundgang unter einer dicken Schneedecke. Die Form des Turms unterstreicht die Ähnlichkeit des Gebäudes mit einem U-Boot, das ins Wasser abtaucht.

La forme serpentine inhabituelle du musée permet aux visiteurs de réaliser un parcours de découverte malgré les tempêtes de neige hivernales. La tour accentue volontairement la similarité avec une tourelle de sous-marin qui se déplacerait sous la surface de la neige.

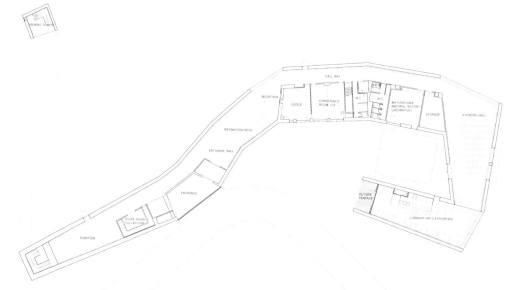

16

MAKOTO SEI WATANABE

MAKOTO SEI WATANABE
1-23-30-2806, Azumabashi
Sumida-ku
Tokyo 130

Tel: + 81 3 38 29 32 21
Fax: + 81 3 38 29 38 37
e-mail: msw@makoto-architect.com
Web: www.makoto-architect.com

Born in 1952 in Yokohama, **MAKOTO SEI WATANABE** attended Yokohama National University from which he graduated with a Master's Degree in Architecture in 1976. He worked from 1979 to 1984 in the office of Arata Isozaki before creating his own firm. His first built work, the Aoyama Technical College, Shibuya, Tokyo (1989), created considerable controversy because of its unusual forms inspired by cartoon graphics. Since that time, Watanabe has worked more and more with computer-generated designs. His work includes: Chronospace, Minato-ku, Tokyo (1991); Mura-no-Terrace gallery, information office and café, Sakauchi Village, Ibi-gun, Gifu (1995); Fiber Wave, environmental art, Gifu and Tokyo (1995–96); Atlas, housing, Suginami-ku, Tokyo (1996); K-Museum, Koto-ku, Tokyo (1996); Fiber Wave, environmental art, The Chicago Athenaeum, Chicago (1998). The Iidabashi Subway Station, Tokyo (2000), the Shin Minamata Shinkansen station (featured here, 2004), and two stations on the Tsukuba Express Line opened in 2005 show his considerable interest in rail facilities. He has also participated extensively in international exhibitions.

SHIN MINAMATA STATION

MINAMATA 2004

FLOOR AREA: 4867 m²
CLIENT: JRTT – Japan Railway Construction,
Transport and Technology Agency
COST: not disclosed

Makoto Sei Watanabe is almost unique among Japanese architects because he has managed to reach into the very closed world of subway and railway station design. One of his most recent efforts was the Shin Minamata station on a newly opened 257-kilometer-long stretch of the Shinkansen "bullet train" lines on the southern island of Kyushu. One reason Watanabe is interested in railway stations is their status as being neither fully closed nor fully open buildings. His design also takes into account the issues of movement with a series of rectangular units that appear to be able to glide back and forth. "The design is a frozen state," he says. "If it were unfrozen, it would move on to the next state. Instead of fixed and finished architecture, it is one moment in a trajectory. The implications extend beyond the design concept. In fact there are plans to extend the platforms after the station opens. Therefore, extensions were provided for unit pieces on the station plaza side and for the structure as a whole. Pieces which are not present when the station opens will emerge at the time of the extension. Unfreezing and restarted movement will occur in the real world, not merely in the realm of virtual thought experiments." Taking up his suggestion that the city should be more closely related to the station, Watanabe was asked to design a sculpture for the station plaza. The work, called "Minamata Mon", is intended to emphasize the ecological concerns of this city made famous by hundreds of cases of methyl mercury poisoning of residents there beginning in 1971. Made of galvanized steel, the sculpture is 7 meters high with a 4 x 4 meter plan. Like much of his work, the piece was generated on a computer using what he calls a "Form Generating + Structural Optimizing" program. Although it is apparently inspired by tree structure, Watanabe insists that "Minamata Mon" "is not a copy of tree form, but is born of a system or program that generates shapes that are akin to life structures."

Unter den Architekten Japans bildet Makoto Sei Watanabe insofern eine Ausnahme, da es ihm gelungen ist, in die bislang sehr konventionelle Welt der Gestaltung von U-Bahn-Stationen und Bahnhöfen vorzudringen. Zu seinen jüngsten Leistungen auf diesem Gebiet gehört der Bahnhof von Shin Minamata an der neu eröffneten, 257 km langen Strecke des Hochgeschwindigkeitszuges Shinkansen auf der Insel Kyushu im Süden Japans. Reizvoll sind Bahnhöfe für Watanabe unter anderem deshalb, weil es sich dabei weder um vollständig geschlossene noch um vollständig offene Gebäude handelt. Mit seinen Entwürfen übersetzte er die Bewegung der Züge in eine Reihe rechtwinkliger Baukörper, die vorwärts und rückwärts zu gleiten scheinen. „Der Bau ist eingefrorene Bewegung", erklärt Watanabe. „Aufgetaut würde er in einen anderen Zustand übergehen. Statt endgültig fix und fertige Architektur zu sein, stellt er die Momentaufnahme einer Fortbewegung dar, deren Implikationen sich über das Entwurfskonzept hinaus fortsetzen. Deshalb sind auch Erweiterungsbauten auf der Seite des Bahnhofsplatzes und Erweiterungen der Gesamtanlage vorgesehen. Bauteile, die zur Zeit der Eröffnung

des Bahnhofs noch nicht existieren, werden später realisiert. Das Auftauen und die wieder einsetzende Bewegung werden also tatsächlich stattfinden – und nicht nur im virtuellen Raum des Gedankenspiels." Watanabe schlug vor, die Stadt enger mit dem Bahnhof zu verknüpfen. Daraufhin erhielt er auch den Auftrag, für den Bahnhofsvorplatz eine Skulptur zu schaffen. Er nannte sie „Minamata Mon". Sie soll die ökologischen Interessen der Stadt Minamata betonen, die 1971 traurige Berühmtheit erlangte, als bei Hunderten von Einwohnern eine Quecksilbervergiftung diagnostiziert wurde. Die 7 m hohe verzinkte Stahlplastik steht auf einer Grundfläche von 4 x 4 m. Wie viele seiner Werke plante Watanabe sie am Computer mit Hilfe eines „formbildenden und strukturell optimierenden" CAD-Programms. Obwohl sie ganz offensichtlich einem Baum nachempfunden ist, besteht Watanabe darauf, dass „Minamata Mon" keine Kopie eines Baums ist, sondern „aus einem formbildenden System oder Programm abgeleitet ist, das naturhaft organische Formen abbildet".

Makoto Sei Watanabe occupe une position unique parmi les architectes japonais car il a réussi à pénétrer le monde très fermé des grands projets de métro et de gares. L'une de ses plus récentes réalisations est celle de Shin Minamata qui dessert une nouvelle section de 257 km de long du Shinkansen – le TGV japonais – récemment ouverte sur l'île méridionale de Kyushu. Une des raisons de son intérêt pour les gares est qu'elles sont des bâtiments ni fermés ni ouverts. Son projet prend également en compte les enjeux de mouvement par une série de longs éléments étroits qui semblent pouvoir coulisser en avant ou en arrière. « Le design est un état figé », dit-il, « s'il n'était pas figé, il se poursuivrait vers un état suivant. Au lieu d'une architecture bloquée et achevée, ce n'est qu'un moment dans une trajectoire. Ces implications vont au-delà du concept. En fait, il existe réellement des plans pour agrandir les quais après l'ouverture de la gare. Ainsi des extensions ont été prévues pour ces éléments du côté de la place de la gare et pour la structure dans son ensemble. Des éléments qui n'existent pas encore à l'ouverture de la gare apparaîtront lors de son extension. Le mouvement libéré redémarrera dans un monde réel, et pas seulement dans celui, virtuel, des expériences. » Sur sa suggestion que la cité soit davantage reliée à la gare, on a demandé à l'architecte de créer une sculpture pour la place de la gare. L'œuvre intitulée « Minamata Mon » veut mettre en avant les préoccupations écologiques de la ville rendue célèbre par des centaines d'empoisonnements au méthyle de mercure survenus en 1971. En acier galvanisé, la sculpture comprise dans un carré de 4 x 4 m mesure 7 m de haut. Comme une grande partie du travail de Watanabe, elle a été dessinée par ordinateur à l'aide d'un logiciel de « génération de formes et d'optimisation structurelle ». Bien qu'elle soit apparemment inspirée d'une structure d'arbre, il insiste sur le fait qu' « il ne s'agit pas d'une copie de forme d'arbre ... elle est née d'un système ou d'un programme qui génère des formes proches de structures vivantes ».

With its slats of varying lengths, the entire Shinkansen platform is flooded with light and accentuates the idea of speed that is already associated with the famous "bullet trains."

Mit seinen unterschiedlich langen Latten erhält der Bahnsteig des Shinkansen reichlich Tageslicht und spiegelt wie ein Abbild die enorme Geschwindigkeit, für die der Zug berühmt ist.

Avec ses éléments en lames de diverses longueurs, la totalité de la gare du Shinkansen est baignée de lumière et renforce l'idée de vitesse associée au fameux train ultrarapide.

Hisatsu Orange Railway

concourse

extension

shelter

station plaza

The streamlined forms of the Shinkansen trains, known for their extreme precision and speed, seem to be in perfect harmony with the white bands of the station itself.
On the following double page, Watanabe's sculpture "Minamata Mon."

Die Stromlinienform der Shinkansen-Züge, die für ihre extreme Präzision und Geschwindigkeit bekannt sind, scheint perfekt mit dem weißen Streifendesign des Bahnsteigs zu harmonieren.
Nächste Doppelseite: Watanabes Plastik „Minamata Mon".

Les formes épurées des trains Shinkansen, connus pour leur extrême précision et leur vitesse, semblent en parfaite harmonie avec les lames blanches de la couverture de la gare.
Double page suivante : une sculpture de Watanabe, « Minamata Mon ».

17

MAKOTO YOKOMIZO

AAT + MAKOTO YOKOMIZO, ARCHITECTS
4 F Insatsukaikan
4-1, Kikuicho
Shinjuku-ku
Tokyo 162-0044

Tel: +81 3 32 05 95 80
Fax: +81 3 32 05 95 89
e-mail: mya@aatplus.com
Web: www.aatplus.com

MAKOTO YOKOMIZO was born in 1962 in Kanagawa. He graduated in 1984 from the Tokyo National University of Fine Arts, Department of Architecture, and completed his Master's degree in the same institution two years later. In 1988, he went to work at Toyo Ito & Associates, remaining there until 2000 and working in particular on the Old People's Home in Yatsushiro, Kumamoto (1994), and the Sendai Médiathèque (2000). In 2001, he created AAT + Makoto Yokomizo Architects. His projects since then have included stage designs for Kota Yamazaki dance performances; Hyper Ballad, New National Theater Tokyo; and Cholon, Theater Cocoon Tokyo, all in 2001. In 2002, he worked on Brussels Kamiya-cho, Tokyo; HEM, Tokyo; and Les Hydropathes, Tokyo. His work in 2003 includes: FUN, Chiba and HAB, Chiba, while in 2004, he worked on three projects: MEM, Chiba; TEM, Tokyo; and MSH, Tokyo. In 2005, he completed the Tomihiro Art Museum, Gunma, featured here. He has been a part-time lecturer at the Tokyo National University of Fine Arts, University of Tokyo, Tokai University, Hosei University, and Tokyo University of Science.

TOMIHIRO ART MUSEUM AZUMA 2003 - 05

FLOOR AREA: 2463 m²
CLIENT: Azuma village, Gunma prefecture
COST: $10.3 million

Located a two-and-half-hours' drive north of Tokyo, the Tomihiro Museum is dedicated to the work of a local poet and illustrator, Tomihiro Hoshino, who is crippled and paints holding a brush in his mouth. First opened in 1991 in a refurbished home for the elderly, the museum attracted more than four million visitors in a period of ten years. An open international competition held in late 2001 to create a new facility drew no fewer than 1211 entries from 53 countries (637 entries from Japan, 574 from abroad). As Makoto Yokomizo says quite modestly, "Our design proposal was selected: a grouping of small circular rooms inspired by soap bubbles." Made up of a series of circles, the design has "been laid out with an eye to their mutual interplay, almost as if trying to solve a puzzle. There was no one guiding principle, no one absolute solution. This compositional 'complementarity' is an important characteristic of the Tomihiro Museum, or what we might call self-optimized design," says Yokomizo. Located on an 18 114 m² site, the Museum has a total floor area of 2463 m². Seeking to break with the typically Modernist grid-type design, Makoto Yokomizo nonetheless makes ample reference to the history of 20th century architecture when he says, "Le Corbusier proposed a Centre for Contemporary Art (Paris, 1931) raised off the ground on pilotis as a prototype of regional 'museums of unlimited growth.' Likewise, Mies van der Rohe's Neue National Gallery (Berlin, 1968) and an earlier proposal for the Bacardi Corporate Headquarters (Santiago de Cuba, 1957) both had a large roof supported on eight columns resting on a basal platform raised off the ground. An overall square shape and raised footprint serves to heighten the abstract quality of the building, as well as to give greater precision to the system. In designing the Tomihiro Art Museum, we ultimately wanted the feeling of a floating building that settled softly to earth on site without sacrificing any of its abstract clarity."

Das zweieinhalb Autostunden nördlich von Tokio gelegene Tomihiro-Museum ist dem Schaffen von Tomihiro Hoshino gewidmet, einem in Gunma lebenden Dichter und Illustrator. Er ist behindert und malt mit dem Mund. Das Museum wurde 1991 zunächst in den Räumen eines umgebauten Seniorenheims eröffnet und verzeichnete in zehn Jahren vier Millionen Besucher. Ende 2001 wurde ein internationaler Wettbewerb ausgelobt, für den nicht weniger als 1211 Entwürfe von Architekten aus 53 Ländern eingereicht wurden (davon 637 aus Japan). Yokomizo meint bescheiden: „Unser Entwurf wurde ausgewählt: eine Zusammenstellung kleiner, runder, von Seifenblasen inspirierter Räume." Den Grundriss aus mehreren Kreisen legte er fast wie ein Puzzle an. „Es gab keine Leitlinien, keine absolute Lösung. Die kompositorische ‚Komplementarität' ist ein wichtiges Charakteristikum des Tomihiro-Museums oder dessen, was man selbst-optimiertes Design nennen könnte", sagte Yokomizo. Das Museumsgelände ist 18 114 m² groß, das

Gebäude hat eine Gesamtgeschossfläche von 2463 m². Zwar brach Yokomizo bewusst mit dem typischen modernen Grundrissraster, bezog sich aber dennoch auf die Baugeschichte des 20. Jahrhunderts, wenn er sagt: „Le Corbusier entwarf ein Zentrum für zeitgenössische Kunst in Paris (1931), das er als Prototyp des regionalen ‚Museums unbegrenzten Wachstums' auf Pilotis stellte. Auch Mies van der Rohes Neue Nationalgalerie in Berlin (1968) und sein früherer Entwurf für den Firmensitz von Bacardi in Santiago de Cuba (1957) haben beide ein großes Dach, das auf acht Säulen ruht, die ihrerseits auf einer erhöhten Sockelplattform stehen. Die Würfelform und die erhöhte Sockelplatte steigern die abstrakte Wirkung des Gebäudes und die konsequente strenge Linie der Gesamtkonstruktion. Mit der Gestaltung des Tomihiro-Museums wollten wir letztlich den Eindruck eines schwebenden Bauwerks erzielen, ohne seine abstrakte Klarheit einzubüßen."

Situé à deux heures et demie de voiture au nord de Tokyo, ce musée est consacré à l'œuvre d'un poète et illustrateur local, Tomihiro Hoshino qui est handicapé et peint en tenant ses brosses entre ses dents. Installé au départ en 1991 dans une maison de retraite réaménagée, le musée a attiré plus de quatre millions de visiteurs en dix ans. Un concours international organisé fin 2001 pour la construction de nouvelles installations a attiré plus de 1211 participants venus de 53 pays, dont 637 du Japon. Comme Makoto Yokomiza le précise avec une certaine modestie : « Il s'agit d'un regroupement de petites salles circulaires inspirées de la forme de bulles de savon. » Le projet « a cherché à multiplier les relations [entre ces cercles] comme s'il s'agissait de résoudre un puzzle. Il n'y avait ni principe fédérateur, ni solution absolue. Cette ‹ complémentarité › dans la composition est ce qui donne à ce musée son importante caractéristique, c'est ce que nous pourrions appeler une conception auto-optimisée ». Implanté sur un terrain de 18 114 m², le bâtiment offre une surface utile totale de 2463 m². Même s'il a cherché à rompre avec la trame moderniste classique, Yokozimo n'en fait pas moins référence à l'histoire de l'architecture du XXe siècle lorsqu'il dit : « Le Corbusier a proposé un Centre d'art contemporain pour Paris en 1931 surélevé sur des pilotis, prototype de ‹ musées de croissance illimitée ›. De même, Mies van der Rohe dans sa Neue Galerie (Berlin, 1968) et dans une proposition antérieure pour le siège de Bacardi (Santiago de Cuba, 1957) avait proposé d'immenses toitures soutenues par huit colonnes reposant sur une plate-forme de basalte qui les isolaient du sol. La forme carrée et la surélévation par rapport au sol mettent ici en valeur le caractère abstrait de ce bâtiment, tout en donnant une plus grande clarté de lecture du système proposé. En concevant le Musée d'art Tomihiro nous cherchions finalement à obtenir une impression de bâtiment flottant, délicatement posé sur le sol sans rien sacrifier de sa clarté abstraite. »

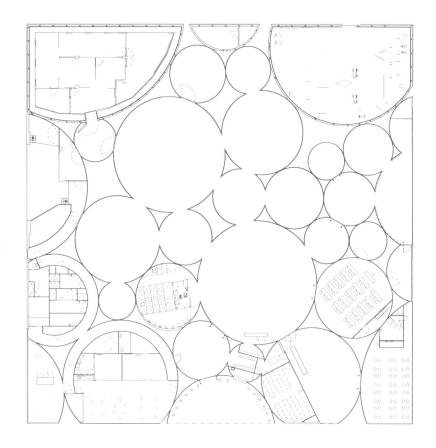

In a sense, the plan of the Tomihiro Museum seems to reverse the design of SANAA's Kanazawa building—inscribing circles in a square instead of the opposite. Reflective surfaces and views of nature from within the building underline its specifically Japanese characteristics.

In gewisser Weise scheint der Grundriss des Tomihiro-Museums den des Museums von SANAA in Kanazawa umzukehren. Hier wurden Kreise in ein Quadrat eingeschrieben und nicht umgekehrt. Spiegelnde Oberflächen und Ausblicke ins Grüne betonen die typischen japanischen Merkmale des Baus.

En un sens, le plan du musée de Tomihiro qui inscrit des cercles dans un carré semble l'inverse du projet de SANAA pour le musée de Kanazawa. Les surfaces réfléchissantes et les vues sur la nature de l'intérieur du bâtiment confirment ses caractéristiques spécifiquement japonaises.

Furniture that might bring to mind some designs of Toyo Ito is used in some spaces, while elsewhere darkened galleries immerse visitors in the atmosphere of the exhibitions. Elevations show the extreme simplicity of the exterior architecture.

In einigen Räumen stehen Möbel, die an Entwürfe von Toyo Ito erinnern; in anderen Bereichen können sich die Besucher in abgedunkelten Galerien ganz auf die Exponate konzentrieren. Die Aufrisse zeigen die äußerste Schlichtheit der Fassaden.

Un mobilier qui pourrait rappeler certains projets de Toyo Ito est utilisé à certains endroits tandis que, partout ailleurs, les galeries sombres plongent les visiteurs dans l'atmosphère des expositions. L'élévation montre l'extrême simplicité des façades.

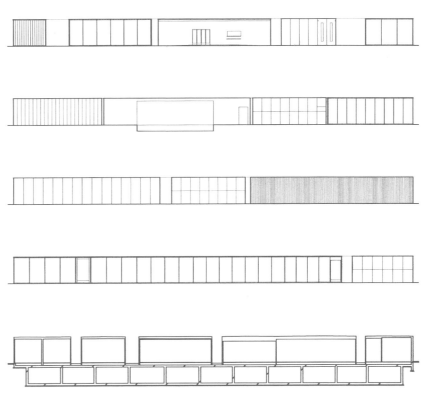

PHOTO CREDITS IMPRINT

CREDITS: PHOTOS / PLANS / DRAWINGS / CAD DOCUMENTS

18-22 bottom © Daici Ano / 22 top, 23 bottom, 25 top © Hitoshi Abe / 23 top-25 bottom © Shinkenchiku-Sha / 26-30 bottom, 31 top, 32-33 © Mitsumasa Fujitsuka / 30 top, 31 bottom, 32 left, 33 right, 37 bottom, 38 bottom, 39 top © Tadao Ando / 35-37 top, 38 top, 39 bottom © Mitsuo Matsuoka / 40-47 © Nacasa & Partners Inc. / 48-52 top, 53 top, 54-58 bottom, 59 © Hiroyuki Hirai / 52 bottom, 53 bottom, 58 top © Shigeru Ban / 60-64 top, 65-67 © Yoshiharu Matsumura / 64 bottom © Shuhei Endo / 68-72 top, 73 © Hiro Sakaguchi AtoZ / 72 bottom © Masaki Endoh and Masahiro Ikeda / 74-78 top, 79 top © Tomio Ohashi / 78 bottom, 79 bottom, 80 bottom, 81 top © Hiroshi Hara / 80 top, 81 bottom-86 top, 87 bottom-89 © Shinkenchiku-Sha / 86 bottom, 87 top © Arata Isozaki / 90-94 bottom, 95 top-97 top and bottom, 98-99 top © TOD'S / 94 top, 95 bottom, 97 middle, 99 bottom, 103 top © Toyo Ito / 101-103 bottom, 104-105 © Hiro Sakaguchi AtoZ / 106-110 top, 111 © Hisao Suzuki / 110 bottom © Waro Kishi / 113-117 © Hiroshi Ueda / 118-123 bottom, 125-127 top, 128 top-131 © Daici Ano / 123 top, 127 bottom, 128 bottom © Kengo Kuma / 132-137 top, 138-139 © Toshiharu Kitajima / 140-144 bottom, 145-149 © Kanazawa Museum / 144 top, 152 top, 153 bottom © SANAA / 151-152 bottom, 153 top © Shinkenchiku-Sha / 154-161 bottom © Toshiharu Kitajima / 161 top © Yoshio Taniguchi / 162-166 top, 167-173 top and bottom © Katsuhisa Kida / 166 bottom, 173 middle © Tezuka Architects /174-183 © Makoto Sei Watanabe/Architects' Office / 184-188 bottom, 189-191 top © Hiro Sakaguchi AtoZ / 188 bottom, 191 bottom © Makoto Yokomizo

To stay informed about upcoming TASCHEN titles, please request our magazine at www.taschen.com/magazine or write to TASCHEN, Hohenzollernring 53, D-50672 Cologne, Germany, contact@taschen.com, Fax: +49-221-254919. We will be happy to send you a free copy of our magazine which is filled with information about all of our books.

© 2006 TASCHEN GmbH
Hohenzollernring 53, D-50672 Köln
www.taschen.com

PROJECT MANAGEMENT: Florian Kobler, Cologne
COLLABORATION: Barbara Huttrop, Cologne
PRODUCTION: Thomas Grell, Cologne
DESIGN: Sense/Net, Andy Disl and Birgit Reber, Cologne
GERMAN TRANSLATION: Annette Wiethüchter, Berlin
FRENCH TRANSLATION: Jacques Bosser, Paris

Printed in Italy
ISBN 3-8228-3988-4